C-813 CAREER EXAMINATION SERIES

*This is your
PASSBOOK for...*

Traffic Device Maintainer

*Test Preparation Study Guide
Questions & Answers*

COPYRIGHT NOTICE

This book is SOLELY intended for, is sold ONLY to, and its use is RESTRICTED to individual, bona fide applicants or candidates who qualify by virtue of having seriously filed applications for appropriate license, certificate, professional and/or promotional advancement, higher school matriculation, scholarship, or other legitimate requirements of education and/or governmental authorities.

This book is NOT intended for use, class instruction, tutoring, training, duplication, copying, reprinting, excerption, or adaptation, etc., by:

1) Other publishers
2) Proprietors and/or Instructors of "Coaching" and/or Preparatory Courses
3) Personnel and/or Training Divisions of commercial, industrial, and governmental organizations
4) Schools, colleges, or universities and/or their departments and staffs, including teachers and other personnel
5) Testing Agencies or Bureaus
6) Study groups which seek by the purchase of a single volume to copy and/or duplicate and/or adapt this material for use by the group as a whole without having purchased individual volumes for each of the members of the group
7) Et al.

Such persons would be in violation of appropriate Federal and State statutes.

PROVISION OF LICENSING AGREEMENTS – Recognized educational, commercial, industrial, and governmental institutions and organizations, and others legitimately engaged in educational pursuits, including training, testing, and measurement activities, may address request for a licensing agreement to the copyright owners, who will determine whether, and under what conditions, including fees and charges, the materials in this book may be used them. In other words, a licensing facility exists for the legitimate use of the material in this book on other than an individual basis. However, it is asseverated and affirmed here that the material in this book CANNOT be used without the receipt of the express permission of such a licensing agreement from the Publishers. Inquiries re licensing should be addressed to the company, attention rights and permissions department.

All rights reserved, including the right of reproduction in whole or in part, in any form or by any means, electronic or mechanical, including photocopying, recording, or by any information storage and retrieval system, without permission in writing from the Publisher.

Copyright © 2025 by
National Learning Corporation

212 Michael Drive, Syosset, NY 11791
(516) 921-8888 • www.passbooks.com
E-mail: info@passbooks.com

PASSBOOK® SERIES

THE *PASSBOOK® SERIES* has been created to prepare applicants and candidates for the ultimate academic battlefield – the examination room.

At some time in our lives, each and every one of us may be required to take an examination – for validation, matriculation, admission, qualification, registration, certification, or licensure.

Based on the assumption that every applicant or candidate has met the basic formal educational standards, has taken the required number of courses, and read the necessary texts, the *PASSBOOK® SERIES* furnishes the one special preparation which may assure passing with confidence, instead of failing with insecurity. Examination questions – together with answers – are furnished as the basic vehicle for study so that the mysteries of the examination and its compounding difficulties may be eliminated or diminished by a sure method.

This book is meant to help you pass your examination provided that you qualify and are serious in your objective.

The entire field is reviewed through the huge store of content information which is succinctly presented through a provocative and challenging approach – the question-and-answer method.

A climate of success is established by furnishing the correct answers at the end of each test.

You soon learn to recognize types of questions, forms of questions, and patterns of questioning. You may even begin to anticipate expected outcomes.

You perceive that many questions are repeated or adapted so that you can gain acute insights, which may enable you to score many sure points.

You learn how to confront new questions, or types of questions, and to attack them confidently and work out the correct answers.

You note objectives and emphases, and recognize pitfalls and dangers, so that you may make positive educational adjustments.

Moreover, you are kept fully informed in relation to new concepts, methods, practices, and directions in the field.

You discover that you are actually taking the examination all the time: you are preparing for the examination by "taking" an examination, not by reading extraneous and/or supererogatory textbooks.

In short, this PASSBOOK®, used directedly, should be an important factor in helping you to pass your test.

TRAFFIC DEVICE MAINTAINER

DUTIES AND RESPONSIBILITIES

Under direct supervision, installs and maintains traffic control devices and markings; performs related work.

EXAMPLES OF TYPICAL TASKS

Prepares, installs, maintains, and repairs traffic control devices, such as signs, stanchions, supports, parking meters, pavement markers, and traffic counters. Operates, maintains, and makes minor adjustments to motor vehicles, marking machines, air compressors, pavement breakers, snow plows, and other field and shop equipment. Performs manual labor in the loading and unloading of trucks, and the placement of traffic devices. Rigs, climbs, and works from ladders and tower trucks in buckets when required. Assists in the routine operation, repair and maintenance of off-street parking facilities and appurtenances. May be assigned to removal of traffic encumbrances. May operate motor vehicles in the performance of assigned duties.

SCOPE OF THE EXAMINATION

The written test will be of the multiple-choice type, and may include questions on: proper use of hand and power tools; arithmetical calculations and making measurements; minor maintenance of automotive and mechanical equipment; reading and interpreting work orders and simple schematics; construction materials and hardware; safe work procedures; and other related areas.

HOW TO TAKE A TEST

I. YOU MUST PASS AN EXAMINATION

A. WHAT EVERY CANDIDATE SHOULD KNOW

Examination applicants often ask us for help in preparing for the written test. What can I study in advance? What kinds of questions will be asked? How will the test be given? How will the papers be graded?

As an applicant for a civil service examination, you may be wondering about some of these things. Our purpose here is to suggest effective methods of advance study and to describe civil service examinations.

Your chances for success on this examination can be increased if you know how to prepare. Those "pre-examination jitters" can be reduced if you know what to expect. You can even experience an adventure in good citizenship if you know why civil service exams are given.

B. WHY ARE CIVIL SERVICE EXAMINATIONS GIVEN?

Civil service examinations are important to you in two ways. As a citizen, you want public jobs filled by employees who know how to do their work. As a job seeker, you want a fair chance to compete for that job on an equal footing with other candidates. The best-known means of accomplishing this two-fold goal is the competitive examination.

Exams are widely publicized throughout the nation. They may be administered for jobs in federal, state, city, municipal, town or village governments or agencies.

Any citizen may apply, with some limitations, such as the age or residence of applicants. Your experience and education may be reviewed to see whether you meet the requirements for the particular examination. When these requirements exist, they are reasonable and applied consistently to all applicants. Thus, a competitive examination may cause you some uneasiness now, but it is your privilege and safeguard.

C. HOW ARE CIVIL SERVICE EXAMS DEVELOPED?

Examinations are carefully written by trained technicians who are specialists in the field known as "psychological measurement," in consultation with recognized authorities in the field of work that the test will cover. These experts recommend the subject matter areas or skills to be tested; only those knowledges or skills important to your success on the job are included. The most reliable books and source materials available are used as references. Together, the experts and technicians judge the difficulty level of the questions.

Test technicians know how to phrase questions so that the problem is clearly stated. Their ethics do not permit "trick" or "catch" questions. Questions may have been tried out on sample groups, or subjected to statistical analysis, to determine their usefulness.

Written tests are often used in combination with performance tests, ratings of training and experience, and oral interviews. All of these measures combine to form the best-known means of finding the right person for the right job.

II. HOW TO PASS THE WRITTEN TEST

A. NATURE OF THE EXAMINATION

To prepare intelligently for civil service examinations, you should know how they differ from school examinations you have taken. In school you were assigned certain definite pages to read or subjects to cover. The examination questions were quite detailed and usually emphasized memory. Civil service exams, on the other hand, try to discover your present ability to perform the duties of a position, plus your potentiality to learn these duties. In other words, a civil service exam attempts to predict how successful you will be. Questions cover such a broad area that they cannot be as minute and detailed as school exam questions.

In the public service similar kinds of work, or positions, are grouped together in one "class." This process is known as *position-classification*. All the positions in a class are paid according to the salary range for that class. One class title covers all of these positions, and they are all tested by the same examination.

B. FOUR BASIC STEPS

1) Study the announcement

How, then, can you know what subjects to study? Our best answer is: "Learn as much as possible about the class of positions for which you've applied." The exam will test the knowledge, skills and abilities needed to do the work.

Your most valuable source of information about the position you want is the official exam announcement. This announcement lists the training and experience qualifications. Check these standards and apply only if you come reasonably close to meeting them.

The brief description of the position in the examination announcement offers some clues to the subjects which will be tested. Think about the job itself. Review the duties in your mind. Can you perform them, or are there some in which you are rusty? Fill in the blank spots in your preparation.

Many jurisdictions preview the written test in the exam announcement by including a section called "Knowledge and Abilities Required," "Scope of the Examination," or some similar heading. Here you will find out specifically what fields will be tested.

2) Review your own background

Once you learn in general what the position is all about, and what you need to know to do the work, ask yourself which subjects you already know fairly well and which need improvement. You may wonder whether to concentrate on improving your strong areas or on building some background in your fields of weakness. When the announcement has specified "some knowledge" or "considerable knowledge," or has used adjectives like "beginning principles of..." or "advanced ... methods," you can get a clue as to the number and difficulty of questions to be asked in any given field. More questions, and hence broader coverage, would be included for those subjects which are more important in the work. Now weigh your strengths and weaknesses against the job requirements and prepare accordingly.

3) Determine the level of the position

Another way to tell how intensively you should prepare is to understand the level of the job for which you are applying. Is it the entering level? In other words, is this the position in which beginners in a field of work are hired? Or is it an intermediate or advanced level? Sometimes this is indicated by such words as "Junior" or "Senior" in the class title. Other jurisdictions use Roman numerals to designate the level – Clerk I, Clerk II, for example. The word "Supervisor" sometimes appears in the title. If the level is not indicated by the title, check the description of duties. Will you be working under very close supervision, or will you have responsibility for independent decisions in this work?

4) Choose appropriate study materials

Now that you know the subjects to be examined and the relative amount of each subject to be covered, you can choose suitable study materials. For beginning level jobs, or even advanced ones, if you have a pronounced weakness in some aspect of your training, read a modern, standard textbook in that field. Be sure it is up to date and has general coverage. Such books are normally available at your library, and the librarian will be glad to help you locate one. For entry-level positions, questions of appropriate difficulty are chosen – neither highly advanced questions, nor those too simple. Such questions require careful thought but not advanced training.

If the position for which you are applying is technical or advanced, you will read more advanced, specialized material. If you are already familiar with the basic principles of your field, elementary textbooks would waste your time. Concentrate on advanced textbooks and technical periodicals. Think through the concepts and review difficult problems in your field.

These are all general sources. You can get more ideas on your own initiative, following these leads. For example, training manuals and publications of the government agency which employs workers in your field can be useful, particularly for technical and professional positions. A letter or visit to the government department involved may result in more specific study suggestions, and certainly will provide you with a more definite idea of the exact nature of the position you are seeking.

III. KINDS OF TESTS

Tests are used for purposes other than measuring knowledge and ability to perform specified duties. For some positions, it is equally important to test ability to make adjustments to new situations or to profit from training. In others, basic mental abilities not dependent on information are essential. Questions which test these things may not appear as pertinent to the duties of the position as those which test for knowledge and information. Yet they are often highly important parts of a fair examination. For very general questions, it is almost impossible to help you direct your study efforts. What we can do is to point out some of the more common of these general abilities needed in public service positions and describe some typical questions.

1) General information

Broad, general information has been found useful for predicting job success in some kinds of work. This is tested in a variety of ways, from vocabulary lists to questions about current events. Basic background in some field of work, such as sociology or economics, may be sampled in a group of questions. Often these are principles which have become familiar to most persons through exposure rather than through formal training. It is difficult to advise you how to study for these questions; being alert to the world around you is our best suggestion.

2) Verbal ability

An example of an ability needed in many positions is verbal or language ability. Verbal ability is, in brief, the ability to use and understand words. Vocabulary and grammar tests are typical measures of this ability. Reading comprehension or paragraph interpretation questions are common in many kinds of civil service tests. You are given a paragraph of written material and asked to find its central meaning.

3) Numerical ability

Number skills can be tested by the familiar arithmetic problem, by checking paired lists of numbers to see which are alike and which are different, or by interpreting charts and graphs. In the latter test, a graph may be printed in the test booklet which you are asked to use as the basis for answering questions.

4) Observation

A popular test for law-enforcement positions is the observation test. A picture is shown to you for several minutes, then taken away. Questions about the picture test your ability to observe both details and larger elements.

5) Following directions

In many positions in the public service, the employee must be able to carry out written instructions dependably and accurately. You may be given a chart with several columns, each column listing a variety of information. The questions require you to carry out directions involving the information given in the chart.

6) Skills and aptitudes

Performance tests effectively measure some manual skills and aptitudes. When the skill is one in which you are trained, such as typing or shorthand, you can practice. These tests are often very much like those given in business school or high school courses. For many of the other skills and aptitudes, however, no short-time preparation can be made. Skills and abilities natural to you or that you have developed throughout your lifetime are being tested.

Many of the general questions just described provide all the data needed to answer the questions and ask you to use your reasoning ability to find the answers. Your best preparation for these tests, as well as for tests of facts and ideas, is to be at your physical and mental best. You, no doubt, have your own methods of getting into an exam-taking mood and keeping "in shape." The next section lists some ideas on this subject.

IV. KINDS OF QUESTIONS

Only rarely is the "essay" question, which you answer in narrative form, used in civil service tests. Civil service tests are usually of the short-answer type. Full instructions for answering these questions will be given to you at the examination. But in case this is your first experience with short-answer questions and separate answer sheets, here is what you need to know:

1) Multiple-choice Questions

Most popular of the short-answer questions is the "multiple choice" or "best answer" question. It can be used, for example, to test for factual knowledge, ability to solve problems or judgment in meeting situations found at work.

A multiple-choice question is normally one of three types—
- It can begin with an incomplete statement followed by several possible endings. You are to find the one ending which *best* completes the statement, although some of the others may not be entirely wrong.
- It can also be a complete statement in the form of a question which is answered by choosing one of the statements listed.

- It can be in the form of a problem – again you select the best answer.

Here is an example of a multiple-choice question with a discussion which should give you some clues as to the method for choosing the right answer:

When an employee has a complaint about his assignment, the action which will *best* help him overcome his difficulty is to
- A. discuss his difficulty with his coworkers
- B. take the problem to the head of the organization
- C. take the problem to the person who gave him the assignment
- D. say nothing to anyone about his complaint

In answering this question, you should study each of the choices to find which is best. Consider choice "A" – Certainly an employee may discuss his complaint with fellow employees, but no change or improvement can result, and the complaint remains unresolved. Choice "B" is a poor choice since the head of the organization probably does not know what assignment you have been given, and taking your problem to him is known as "going over the head" of the supervisor. The supervisor, or person who made the assignment, is the person who can clarify it or correct any injustice. Choice "C" is, therefore, correct. To say nothing, as in choice "D," is unwise. Supervisors have and interest in knowing the problems employees are facing, and the employee is seeking a solution to his problem.

2) True/False Questions

The "true/false" or "right/wrong" form of question is sometimes used. Here a complete statement is given. Your job is to decide whether the statement is right or wrong.

SAMPLE: A roaming cell-phone call to a nearby city costs less than a non-roaming call to a distant city.

This statement is wrong, or false, since roaming calls are more expensive.

This is not a complete list of all possible question forms, although most of the others are variations of these common types. You will always get complete directions for answering questions. Be sure you understand *how* to mark your answers – ask questions until you do.

V. RECORDING YOUR ANSWERS

Computer terminals are used more and more today for many different kinds of exams.
For an examination with very few applicants, you may be told to record your answers in the test booklet itself. Separate answer sheets are much more common. If this separate answer sheet is to be scored by machine – and this is often the case – it is highly important that you mark your answers correctly in order to get credit.

An electronic scoring machine is often used in civil service offices because of the speed with which papers can be scored. Machine-scored answer sheets must be marked with a pencil, which will be given to you. This pencil has a high graphite content which responds to the electronic scoring machine. As a matter of fact, stray dots may register as answers, so do not let your pencil rest on the answer sheet while you are pondering the correct answer. Also, if your pencil lead breaks or is otherwise defective, ask for another.

Since the answer sheet will be dropped in a slot in the scoring machine, be careful not to bend the corners or get the paper crumpled.

The answer sheet normally has five vertical columns of numbers, with 30 numbers to a column. These numbers correspond to the question numbers in your test booklet. After each number, going across the page are four or five pairs of dotted lines. These short dotted lines have small letters or numbers above them. The first two pairs may also have a "T" or "F" above the letters. This indicates that the first two pairs only are to be used if the questions are of the true-false type. If the questions are multiple choice, disregard the "T" and "F" and pay attention only to the small letters or numbers.

Answer your questions in the manner of the sample that follows:

32. The largest city in the United States is
    A. Washington, D.C.
    B. New York City
    C. Chicago
    D. Detroit
    E. San Francisco

1) Choose the answer you think is best. (New York City is the largest, so "B" is correct.)
2) Find the row of dotted lines numbered the same as the question you are answering. (Find row number 32)
3) Find the pair of dotted lines corresponding to the answer. (Find the pair of lines under the mark "B.")
4) Make a solid black mark between the dotted lines.

VI. BEFORE THE TEST

Common sense will help you find procedures to follow to get ready for an examination. Too many of us, however, overlook these sensible measures. Indeed, nervousness and fatigue have been found to be the most serious reasons why applicants fail to do their best on civil service tests. Here is a list of reminders:

- Begin your preparation early – Don't wait until the last minute to go scurrying around for books and materials or to find out what the position is all about.
- Prepare continuously – An hour a night for a week is better than an all-night cram session. This has been definitely established. What is more, a night a week for a month will return better dividends than crowding your study into a shorter period of time.
- Locate the place of the exam – You have been sent a notice telling you when and where to report for the examination. If the location is in a different town or otherwise unfamiliar to you, it would be well to inquire the best route and learn something about the building.
- Relax the night before the test – Allow your mind to rest. Do not study at all that night. Plan some mild recreation or diversion; then go to bed early and get a good night's sleep.
- Get up early enough to make a leisurely trip to the place for the test – This way unforeseen events, traffic snarls, unfamiliar buildings, etc. will not upset you.
- Dress comfortably – A written test is not a fashion show. You will be known by number and not by name, so wear something comfortable.

- Leave excess paraphernalia at home – Shopping bags and odd bundles will get in your way. You need bring only the items mentioned in the official notice you received; usually everything you need is provided. Do not bring reference books to the exam. They will only confuse those last minutes and be taken away from you when in the test room.
- Arrive somewhat ahead of time – If because of transportation schedules you must get there very early, bring a newspaper or magazine to take your mind off yourself while waiting.
- Locate the examination room – When you have found the proper room, you will be directed to the seat or part of the room where you will sit. Sometimes you are given a sheet of instructions to read while you are waiting. Do not fill out any forms until you are told to do so; just read them and be prepared.
- Relax and prepare to listen to the instructions
- If you have any physical problem that may keep you from doing your best, be sure to tell the test administrator. If you are sick or in poor health, you really cannot do your best on the exam. You can come back and take the test some other time.

VII. AT THE TEST

The day of the test is here and you have the test booklet in your hand. The temptation to get going is very strong. Caution! There is more to success than knowing the right answers. You must know how to identify your papers and understand variations in the type of short-answer question used in this particular examination. Follow these suggestions for maximum results from your efforts:

1) Cooperate with the monitor

The test administrator has a duty to create a situation in which you can be as much at ease as possible. He will give instructions, tell you when to begin, check to see that you are marking your answer sheet correctly, and so on. He is not there to guard you, although he will see that your competitors do not take unfair advantage. He wants to help you do your best.

2) Listen to all instructions

Don't jump the gun! Wait until you understand all directions. In most civil service tests you get more time than you need to answer the questions. So don't be in a hurry. Read each word of instructions until you clearly understand the meaning. Study the examples, listen to all announcements and follow directions. Ask questions if you do not understand what to do.

3) Identify your papers

Civil service exams are usually identified by number only. You will be assigned a number; you must not put your name on your test papers. Be sure to copy your number correctly. Since more than one exam may be given, copy your exact examination title.

4) Plan your time

Unless you are told that a test is a "speed" or "rate of work" test, speed itself is usually not important. Time enough to answer all the questions will be provided, but this does not mean that you have all day. An overall time limit has been set. Divide the total time (in minutes) by the number of questions to determine the approximate time you have for each question.

5) Do not linger over difficult questions

If you come across a difficult question, mark it with a paper clip (useful to have along) and come back to it when you have been through the booklet. One caution if you do this – be sure to skip a number on your answer sheet as well. Check often to be sure that you have not lost your place and that you are marking in the row numbered the same as the question you are answering.

6) Read the questions

Be sure you know what the question asks! Many capable people are unsuccessful because they failed to *read* the questions correctly.

7) Answer all questions

Unless you have been instructed that a penalty will be deducted for incorrect answers, it is better to guess than to omit a question.

8) Speed tests

It is often better NOT to guess on speed tests. It has been found that on timed tests people are tempted to spend the last few seconds before time is called in marking answers at random – without even reading them – in the hope of picking up a few extra points. To discourage this practice, the instructions may warn you that your score will be "corrected" for guessing. That is, a penalty will be applied. The incorrect answers will be deducted from the correct ones, or some other penalty formula will be used.

9) Review your answers

If you finish before time is called, go back to the questions you guessed or omitted to give them further thought. Review other answers if you have time.

10) Return your test materials

If you are ready to leave before others have finished or time is called, take ALL your materials to the monitor and leave quietly. Never take any test material with you. The monitor can discover whose papers are not complete, and taking a test booklet may be grounds for disqualification.

VIII. EXAMINATION TECHNIQUES

1) Read the general instructions carefully. These are usually printed on the first page of the exam booklet. As a rule, these instructions refer to the timing of the examination; the fact that you should not start work until the signal and must stop work at a signal, etc. If there are any *special* instructions, such as a choice of questions to be answered, make sure that you note this instruction carefully.

2) When you are ready to start work on the examination, that is as soon as the signal has been given, read the instructions to each question booklet, underline any key words or phrases, such as *least, best, outline, describe* and the like. In this way you will tend to answer as requested rather than discover on reviewing your paper that you *listed without describing*, that you selected the *worst* choice rather than the *best* choice, etc.

3) If the examination is of the objective or multiple-choice type – that is, each question will also give a series of possible answers: A, B, C or D, and you are called upon to select the best answer and write the letter next to that answer on your answer paper – it is advisable to start answering each question in turn. There may be anywhere from 50 to 100 such questions in the three or four hours allotted and you can see how much time would be taken if you read through all the questions before beginning to answer any. Furthermore, if you come across a question or group of questions which you know would be difficult to answer, it would undoubtedly affect your handling of all the other questions.

4) If the examination is of the essay type and contains but a few questions, it is a moot point as to whether you should read all the questions before starting to answer any one. Of course, if you are given a choice – say five out of seven and the like – then it is essential to read all the questions so you can eliminate the two that are most difficult. If, however, you are asked to answer all the questions, there may be danger in trying to answer the easiest one first because you may find that you will spend too much time on it. The best technique is to answer the first question, then proceed to the second, etc.

5) Time your answers. Before the exam begins, write down the time it started, then add the time allowed for the examination and write down the time it must be completed, then divide the time available somewhat as follows:
    - If 3-1/2 hours are allowed, that would be 210 minutes. If you have 80 objective-type questions, that would be an average of 2-1/2 minutes per question. Allow yourself no more than 2 minutes per question, or a total of 160 minutes, which will permit about 50 minutes to review.
    - If for the time allotment of 210 minutes there are 7 essay questions to answer, that would average about 30 minutes a question. Give yourself only 25 minutes per question so that you have about 35 minutes to review.

6) The most important instruction is to *read each question* and make sure you know what is wanted. The second most important instruction is to *time yourself properly* so that you answer every question. The third most important instruction is to *answer every question*. Guess if you have to but include something for each question. Remember that you will receive no credit for a blank and will probably receive some credit if you write something in answer to an essay question. If you guess a letter – say "B" for a multiple-choice question – you may have guessed right. If you leave a blank as an answer to a multiple-choice question, the examiners may respect your feelings but it will not add a point to your score. Some exams may penalize you for wrong answers, so in such cases *only*, you may not want to guess unless you have some basis for your answer.

7) Suggestions
   a. Objective-type questions
      1. Examine the question booklet for proper sequence of pages and questions
      2. Read all instructions carefully
      3. Skip any question which seems too difficult; return to it after all other questions have been answered
      4. Apportion your time properly; do not spend too much time on any single question or group of questions

5. Note and underline key words – *all, most, fewest, least, best, worst, same, opposite*, etc.
6. Pay particular attention to negatives
7. Note unusual option, e.g., unduly long, short, complex, different or similar in content to the body of the question
8. Observe the use of "hedging" words – *probably, may, most likely*, etc.
9. Make sure that your answer is put next to the same number as the question
10. Do not second-guess unless you have good reason to believe the second answer is definitely more correct
11. Cross out original answer if you decide another answer is more accurate; do not erase until you are ready to hand your paper in
12. Answer all questions; guess unless instructed otherwise
13. Leave time for review

  b. Essay questions
    1. Read each question carefully
    2. Determine exactly what is wanted. Underline key words or phrases.
    3. Decide on outline or paragraph answer
    4. Include many different points and elements unless asked to develop any one or two points or elements
    5. Show impartiality by giving pros and cons unless directed to select one side only
    6. Make and write down any assumptions you find necessary to answer the questions
    7. Watch your English, grammar, punctuation and choice of words
    8. Time your answers; don't crowd material

8) Answering the essay question

Most essay questions can be answered by framing the specific response around several key words or ideas. Here are a few such key words or ideas:

M's: manpower, materials, methods, money, management
P's: purpose, program, policy, plan, procedure, practice, problems, pitfalls, personnel, public relations

  a. Six basic steps in handling problems:
    1. Preliminary plan and background development
    2. Collect information, data and facts
    3. Analyze and interpret information, data and facts
    4. Analyze and develop solutions as well as make recommendations
    5. Prepare report and sell recommendations
    6. Install recommendations and follow up effectiveness

  b. Pitfalls to avoid
    1. *Taking things for granted* – A statement of the situation does not necessarily imply that each of the elements is necessarily true; for example, a complaint may be invalid and biased so that all that can be taken for granted is that a complaint has been registered

2. *Considering only one side of a situation* – Wherever possible, indicate several alternatives and then point out the reasons you selected the best one
3. *Failing to indicate follow up* – Whenever your answer indicates action on your part, make certain that you will take proper follow-up action to see how successful your recommendations, procedures or actions turn out to be
4. *Taking too long in answering any single question* – Remember to time your answers properly

IX. AFTER THE TEST

Scoring procedures differ in detail among civil service jurisdictions although the general principles are the same. Whether the papers are hand-scored or graded by machine we have described, they are nearly always graded by number. That is, the person who marks the paper knows only the number – never the name – of the applicant. Not until all the papers have been graded will they be matched with names. If other tests, such as training and experience or oral interview ratings have been given, scores will be combined. Different parts of the examination usually have different weights. For example, the written test might count 60 percent of the final grade, and a rating of training and experience 40 percent. In many jurisdictions, veterans will have a certain number of points added to their grades.

After the final grade has been determined, the names are placed in grade order and an eligible list is established. There are various methods for resolving ties between those who get the same final grade – probably the most common is to place first the name of the person whose application was received first. Job offers are made from the eligible list in the order the names appear on it. You will be notified of your grade and your rank as soon as all these computations have been made. This will be done as rapidly as possible.

People who are found to meet the requirements in the announcement are called "eligibles." Their names are put on a list of eligible candidates. An eligible's chances of getting a job depend on how high he stands on this list and how fast agencies are filling jobs from the list.

When a job is to be filled from a list of eligibles, the agency asks for the names of people on the list of eligibles for that job. When the civil service commission receives this request, it sends to the agency the names of the three people highest on this list. Or, if the job to be filled has specialized requirements, the office sends the agency the names of the top three persons who meet these requirements from the general list.

The appointing officer makes a choice from among the three people whose names were sent to him. If the selected person accepts the appointment, the names of the others are put back on the list to be considered for future openings.

That is the rule in hiring from all kinds of eligible lists, whether they are for typist, carpenter, chemist, or something else. For every vacancy, the appointing officer has his choice of any one of the top three eligibles on the list. This explains why the person whose name is on top of the list sometimes does not get an appointment when some of the persons lower on the list do. If the appointing officer chooses the second or third eligible, the No. 1 eligible does not get a job at once, but stays on the list until he is appointed or the list is terminated.

X. HOW TO PASS THE INTERVIEW TEST

The examination for which you applied requires an oral interview test. You have already taken the written test and you are now being called for the interview test – the final part of the formal examination.

You may think that it is not possible to prepare for an interview test and that there are no procedures to follow during an interview. Our purpose is to point out some things you can do in advance that will help you and some good rules to follow and pitfalls to avoid while you are being interviewed.

What is an interview supposed to test?

The written examination is designed to test the technical knowledge and competence of the candidate; the oral is designed to evaluate intangible qualities, not readily measured otherwise, and to establish a list showing the relative fitness of each candidate – as measured against his competitors – for the position sought. Scoring is not on the basis of "right" and "wrong," but on a sliding scale of values ranging from "not passable" to "outstanding." As a matter of fact, it is possible to achieve a relatively low score without a single "incorrect" answer because of evident weakness in the qualities being measured.

Occasionally, an examination may consist entirely of an oral test – either an individual or a group oral. In such cases, information is sought concerning the technical knowledges and abilities of the candidate, since there has been no written examination for this purpose. More commonly, however, an oral test is used to supplement a written examination.

Who conducts interviews?

The composition of oral boards varies among different jurisdictions. In nearly all, a representative of the personnel department serves as chairman. One of the members of the board may be a representative of the department in which the candidate would work. In some cases, "outside experts" are used, and, frequently, a businessman or some other representative of the general public is asked to serve. Labor and management or other special groups may be represented. The aim is to secure the services of experts in the appropriate field.

However the board is composed, it is a good idea (and not at all improper or unethical) to ascertain in advance of the interview who the members are and what groups they represent. When you are introduced to them, you will have some idea of their backgrounds and interests, and at least you will not stutter and stammer over their names.

What should be done before the interview?

While knowledge about the board members is useful and takes some of the surprise element out of the interview, there is other preparation which is more substantive. It *is* possible to prepare for an oral interview – in several ways:

1) Keep a copy of your application and review it carefully before the interview

This may be the only document before the oral board, and the starting point of the interview. Know what education and experience you have listed there, and the sequence and dates of all of it. Sometimes the board will ask you to review the highlights of your experience for them; you should not have to hem and haw doing it.

2) Study the class specification and the examination announcement

Usually, the oral board has one or both of these to guide them. The qualities, characteristics or knowledges required by the position sought are stated in these documents. They offer valuable clues as to the nature of the oral interview. For example, if the job involves supervisory responsibilities, the announcement will usually indicate that knowledge of modern supervisory methods and the qualifications of the candidate as a supervisor will be tested. If so, you can expect such questions, frequently in the form of a hypothetical situation which you are expected to solve. NEVER go into an oral without knowledge of the duties and responsibilities of the job you seek.

3) Think through each qualification required

Try to visualize the kind of questions you would ask if you were a board member. How well could you answer them? Try especially to appraise your own knowledge and background in each area, *measured against the job sought*, and identify any areas in which you are weak. Be critical and realistic – do not flatter yourself.

4) Do some general reading in areas in which you feel you may be weak

For example, if the job involves supervision and your past experience has NOT, some general reading in supervisory methods and practices, particularly in the field of human relations, might be useful. Do NOT study agency procedures or detailed manuals. The oral board will be testing your understanding and capacity, not your memory.

5) Get a good night's sleep and watch your general health and mental attitude

You will want a clear head at the interview. Take care of a cold or any other minor ailment, and of course, no hangovers.

What should be done on the day of the interview?

Now comes the day of the interview itself. Give yourself plenty of time to get there. Plan to arrive somewhat ahead of the scheduled time, particularly if your appointment is in the fore part of the day. If a previous candidate fails to appear, the board might be ready for you a bit early. By early afternoon an oral board is almost invariably behind schedule if there are many candidates, and you may have to wait. Take along a book or magazine to read, or your application to review, but leave any extraneous material in the waiting room when you go in for your interview. In any event, relax and compose yourself.

The matter of dress is important. The board is forming impressions about you – from your experience, your manners, your attitude, and your appearance. Give your personal appearance careful attention. Dress your best, but not your flashiest. Choose conservative, appropriate clothing, and be sure it is immaculate. This is a business interview, and your appearance should indicate that you regard it as such. Besides, being well groomed and properly dressed will help boost your confidence.

Sooner or later, someone will call your name and escort you into the interview room. *This is it.* From here on you are on your own. It is too late for any more preparation. But remember, you asked for this opportunity to prove your fitness, and you are here because your request was granted.

What happens when you go in?

The usual sequence of events will be as follows: The clerk (who is often the board stenographer) will introduce you to the chairman of the oral board, who will introduce you to the other members of the board. Acknowledge the introductions before you sit down. Do not be surprised if you find a microphone facing you or a stenotypist sitting by. Oral interviews are usually recorded in the event of an appeal or other review.

Usually the chairman of the board will open the interview by reviewing the highlights of your education and work experience from your application – primarily for the benefit of the other members of the board, as well as to get the material into the record. Do not interrupt or comment unless there is an error or significant misinterpretation; if that is the case, do not hesitate. But do not quibble about insignificant matters. Also, he will usually ask you some question about your education, experience or your present job – partly to get you to start talking and to establish the interviewing "rapport." He may start the actual questioning, or turn it over to one of the other members. Frequently, each member undertakes the questioning on a particular area, one in which he is perhaps most competent, so you can expect each member to participate in the examination. Because time is limited, you may also expect some rather abrupt switches in the direction the questioning takes, so do not be upset by it. Normally, a board member will not pursue a single line of questioning unless he discovers a particular strength or weakness.

After each member has participated, the chairman will usually ask whether any member has any further questions, then will ask you if you have anything you wish to add. Unless you are expecting this question, it may floor you. Worse, it may start you off on an extended, extemporaneous speech. The board is not usually seeking more information. The question is principally to offer you a last opportunity to present further qualifications or to indicate that you have nothing to add. So, if you feel that a significant qualification or characteristic has been overlooked, it is proper to point it out in a sentence or so. Do not compliment the board on the thoroughness of their examination – they have been sketchy, and you know it. If you wish, merely say, "No thank you, I have nothing further to add." This is a point where you can "talk yourself out" of a good impression or fail to present an important bit of information. Remember, *you close the interview yourself*.

The chairman will then say, "That is all, Mr. _____, thank you." Do not be startled; the interview is over, and quicker than you think. Thank him, gather your belongings and take your leave. Save your sigh of relief for the other side of the door.

How to put your best foot forward

Throughout this entire process, you may feel that the board individually and collectively is trying to pierce your defenses, seek out your hidden weaknesses and embarrass and confuse you. Actually, this is not true. They are obliged to make an appraisal of your qualifications for the job you are seeking, and they want to see you in your best light. Remember, they must interview all candidates and a non-cooperative candidate may become a failure in spite of their best efforts to bring out his qualifications. Here are 15 suggestions that will help you:

1) Be natural – Keep your attitude confident, not cocky

If you are not confident that you can do the job, do not expect the board to be. Do not apologize for your weaknesses, try to bring out your strong points. The board is interested in a positive, not negative, presentation. Cockiness will antagonize any board member and make him wonder if you are covering up a weakness by a false show of strength.

2) Get comfortable, but don't lounge or sprawl

Sit erectly but not stiffly. A careless posture may lead the board to conclude that you are careless in other things, or at least that you are not impressed by the importance of the occasion. Either conclusion is natural, even if incorrect. Do not fuss with your clothing, a pencil or an ashtray. Your hands may occasionally be useful to emphasize a point; do not let them become a point of distraction.

3) Do not wisecrack or make small talk

This is a serious situation, and your attitude should show that you consider it as such. Further, the time of the board is limited – they do not want to waste it, and neither should you.

4) Do not exaggerate your experience or abilities
In the first place, from information in the application or other interviews and sources, the board may know more about you than you think. Secondly, you probably will not get away with it. An experienced board is rather adept at spotting such a situation, so do not take the chance.

5) If you know a board member, do not make a point of it, yet do not hide it
Certainly you are not fooling him, and probably not the other members of the board. Do not try to take advantage of your acquaintanceship – it will probably do you little good.

6) Do not dominate the interview
Let the board do that. They will give you the clues – do not assume that you have to do all the talking. Realize that the board has a number of questions to ask you, and do not try to take up all the interview time by showing off your extensive knowledge of the answer to the first one.

7) Be attentive
You only have 20 minutes or so, and you should keep your attention at its sharpest throughout. When a member is addressing a problem or question to you, give him your undivided attention. Address your reply principally to him, but do not exclude the other board members.

8) Do not interrupt
A board member may be stating a problem for you to analyze. He will ask you a question when the time comes. Let him state the problem, and wait for the question.

9) Make sure you understand the question
Do not try to answer until you are sure what the question is. If it is not clear, restate it in your own words or ask the board member to clarify it for you. However, do not haggle about minor elements.

10) Reply promptly but not hastily
A common entry on oral board rating sheets is "candidate responded readily," or "candidate hesitated in replies." Respond as promptly and quickly as you can, but do not jump to a hasty, ill-considered answer.

11) Do not be peremptory in your answers
A brief answer is proper – but do not fire your answer back. That is a losing game from your point of view. The board member can probably ask questions much faster than you can answer them.

12) Do not try to create the answer you think the board member wants
He is interested in what kind of mind you have and how it works – not in playing games. Furthermore, he can usually spot this practice and will actually grade you down on it.

13) Do not switch sides in your reply merely to agree with a board member
Frequently, a member will take a contrary position merely to draw you out and to see if you are willing and able to defend your point of view. Do not start a debate, yet do not surrender a good position. If a position is worth taking, it is worth defending.

14) Do not be afraid to admit an error in judgment if you are shown to be wrong

The board knows that you are forced to reply without any opportunity for careful consideration. Your answer may be demonstrably wrong. If so, admit it and get on with the interview.

15) Do not dwell at length on your present job

The opening question may relate to your present assignment. Answer the question but do not go into an extended discussion. You are being examined for a *new* job, not your present one. As a matter of fact, try to phrase ALL your answers in terms of the job for which you are being examined.

Basis of Rating

Probably you will forget most of these "do's" and "don'ts" when you walk into the oral interview room. Even remembering them all will not ensure you a passing grade. Perhaps you did not have the qualifications in the first place. But remembering them will help you to put your best foot forward, without treading on the toes of the board members.

Rumor and popular opinion to the contrary notwithstanding, an oral board wants you to make the best appearance possible. They know you are under pressure – but they also want to see how you respond to it as a guide to what your reaction would be under the pressures of the job you seek. They will be influenced by the degree of poise you display, the personal traits you show and the manner in which you respond.

ABOUT THIS BOOK

This book contains tests divided into Examination Sections. Go through each test, answering every question in the margin. We have also attached a sample answer sheet at the back of the book that can be removed and used. At the end of each test look at the answer key and check your answers. On the ones you got wrong, look at the right answer choice and learn. Do not fill in the answers first. Do not memorize the questions and answers, but understand the answer and principles involved. On your test, the questions will likely be different from the samples. Questions are changed and new ones added. If you understand these past questions you should have success with any changes that arise. Tests may consist of several types of questions. We have additional books on each subject should more study be advisable or necessary for you. Finally, the more you study, the better prepared you will be. This book is intended to be the last thing you study before you walk into the examination room. Prior study of relevant texts is also recommended. NLC publishes some of these in our Fundamental Series. Knowledge and good sense are important factors in passing your exam. Good luck also helps. So now study this Passbook, absorb the material contained within and take that knowledge into the examination. Then do your best to pass that exam.

EXAMINATION SECTION

EXAMINATION SECTION
TEST 1

DIRECTIONS: Each question or incomplete statement is followed by several suggested answers or completions. Select the one that BEST answers the question or completes the statement. *PRINT THE LETTER OF THE CORRECT ANSWER IN THE SPACE AT THE RIGHT.*

1. In a hand tap set, the tap used to start a thread in a drilled hole is known as a _____ tap.   1._____

    A. taper B. plug C. small D. bottoming

2. The type of fastener used to fasten thin gauge metal to wood backing, without drilling, is known as a   2._____

    A. sheet metal screw
    B. cap screw
    C. wood screw
    D. screw nail

3. Set screws are usually used for   3._____

    A. fastening collars to shafts
    B. holding thin metal sheets together
    C. holding roller bearings to shafts
    D. clamping together steel angles

4. When using a pedestal type grinding wheel, the operator should always   4._____

    A. have the work-rest loose
    B. avoid striking the rotating wheel
    C. increase the speed above normal
    D. use a respirator

5. A flat cold chisel is the type of chisel usually used for chipping and/or cutting   5._____

    A. filleted corners
    B. flat surfaces
    C. V-shaped grooves
    D. narrow grooves

6. The type of chisel that is usually used to cut keyways in cast iron is generally known as a _____ chisel.   6._____

    A. star
    B. cold
    C. cape
    D. diamond point

7. The primary difference between brazing and soldering is that brazing requires   7._____

    A. greater heat
    B. a smaller soldering iron
    C. the use of soft solder
    D. the use of 50-50 solder

Questions 8-9.

DIRECTIONS: Questions 8 and 9 refer to the sketch below.

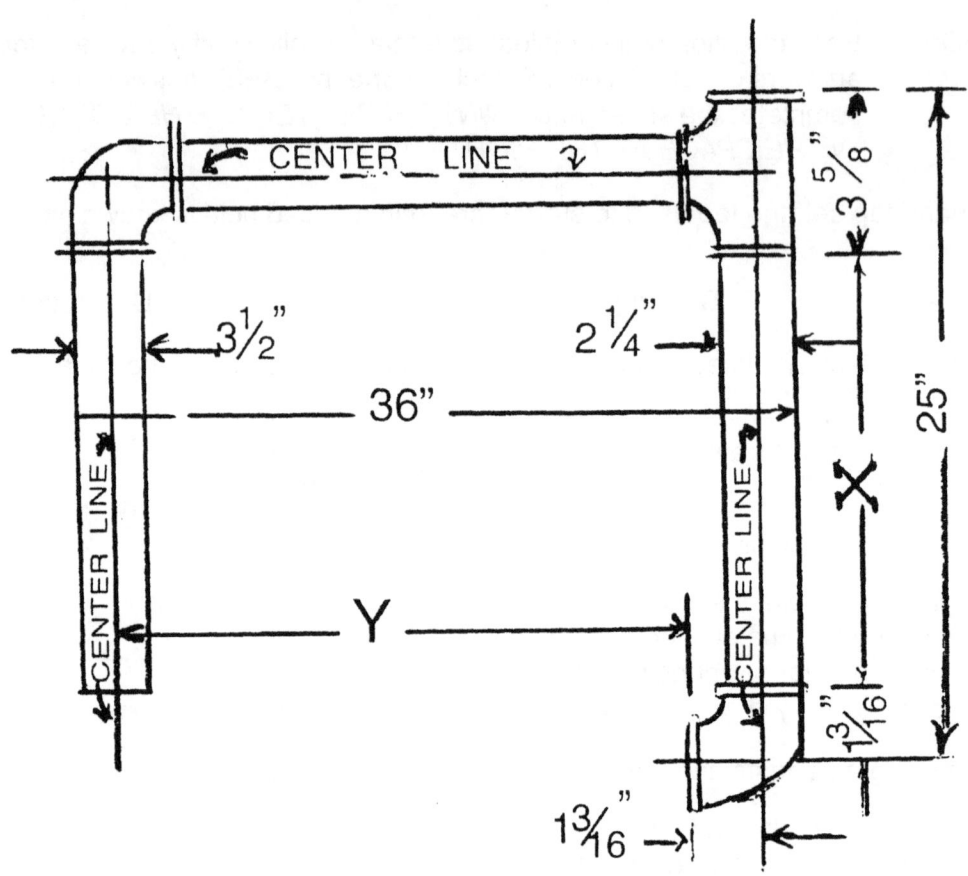

8. In the above sketch, the dimension X, in inches, is 8.___

   A. 19 13/16   B. 20 3/16   C. 20 3/8   D. 21 3/16

9. In the above sketch, the dimension Y, in inches, is 9.___

   A. 30 7/16   B. 31 5/16   C. 31 7/16   D. 31 15/16

10. A piece of 4" cast iron pipe may BEST be cut with a 10.___

    A. hacksaw having a blade with 32 teeth per inch
    B. hacksaw having a blade with 14 teeth per inch
    C. hammer and round nose chisel
    D. hammer and diamond point chisel

11. A four-inch length of straight pipe, threaded on both ends, is generally called a 11.___

    A. sleeve   B. nipple   C. stud   D. extension

12. A pipe fitting that is usually used to join together two threaded pipes of the same diameter is known as a 12.___

    A. union
    B. straight T with reducer leg
    C. nipple
    D. straight tee

13. A pipe fitting that is generally used to join two threaded pipes of different diameters is 13._____
called a(n)

 A. close nipple B. union
 C. adapter D. reducer

14. A 90° pipe fitting that has a male thread at one end and a female thread at the other end 14._____
is generally known as a 90°

 A. elbow B. street elbow
 C. reducing ell D. long radius ell

15. Paints generally used for covering outside pipes or sheet iron are composed of 15._____

 A. mineral pigments, organic vehicles and thinners
 B. resins dissolved in organic thinners
 C. pigmented oil and linseed oil
 D. lac gum dissolved in alcohol

16. A painted panel of wood after being exposed to the atmosphere becomes leather-like in 16._____
appearance.
This paint failure is called

 A. checking B. alligatoring
 C. wrinkling D. chalking

17. Paint brushes that are used for alkyd paints are usually cleaned with 17._____

 A. soap and water
 B. turpentine and mineral spirits
 C. linseed oil
 D. denatured alcohol mixed with water

18. Of the following statements, the one which is INCORRECT concerning painting practices 18._____
is:

 A. Zinc dust primers are used for galvanized iron and sheet zinc
 B. Red lead paint is usually used as a final coat for steel surfaces
 C. Rubber-base paints may be applied to dry or damp walls
 D. Freshly varnished work should be kept clean and in a dust-free space

19. A white paint, that can cover 500 square feet of surface per gallon, is used to paint the 19._____
crosswalks at street intersections.
If the area at each intersection is equal to 300 square feet, the number of gallons
required to paint 50 intersections is MOST NEARLY

 A. 10 B. 20 C. 30 D. 40

20. Of the following methods of splicing insulated electrical wires, the one which is recom- 20._____
mended is to strip the ends, twist them together,

 A. and cover with friction tape
 B. solder and cover with friction tape
 C. shellac and cover with rubber tape
 D. solder, cover with rubber tape, and then with friction tape

21. If two 120V incandescent lamps are connected in parallel in a 120V circuit, the result will MOST likely be that the

    A. lamps will light up to normal brilliancy
    B. voltage across each lamp will be reduced to 60 volts
    C. life of each lamp will be doubled
    D. lamp will light up to 1/2 their normal brilliancy

22. Portable electric hand tools are usually polarized by means of a(n)

    A. circuit breaker   B. fuse
    C. three-prong plug   D. overload switch

23. The flux generally used when soldering electrical copper connections is

    A. zinc chloride
    B. an alcoholic solution of resin
    C. muriatic acid
    D. stearin

24. Fuses in the electric wiring systems of a car or truck are MAINLY used for the purpose of

    A. making it easy to disconnect some of the lights while allowing others to burn
    B. reducing the amount of current used, in order to save the battery
    C. automatically opening the circuit in case of an overload
    D. preventing the battery from overcharging under high speed

25. The BEST way to fasten electric conduit to an outlet box is by means of a

    A. bushing on the end of the conduit
    B. locknut on the outside of the box
    C. bushing on the inside and a locknut on the outside
    D. locknut on the inside and a bushing on the outside

26. The GREATEST hazard of explosion exists whenever

    A. gasoline is stored in airtight tanks
    B. a pool of gasoline is exposed to air
    C. gasoline is in a partially-full closed tank
    D. gasoline comes into contact with oil

27. In the above sketch, the head of a screw which represents an alien-head screw is numbered

    A. 1   B. 2   C. 3   D. 4

28. A ratchet wrench is usually used when

   A. the surface finish of a bolt must be preserved
   B. only a short swing of the wrench handle is permissible
   C. nuts are practically inaccessible
   D. tightening compression fittings

29. Grout in construction work is usually used to

   A. increase the strength of concrete
   B. seal porous timber surfaces
   C. prime concrete sidewalks
   D. fill spaces between brick or stone joints

30. A cutting tool that is being ground on an emery wheel is usually cooled by immersing it in

   A. oil
   B. water
   C. kerosene
   D. turpentine

31. Of the following statements concerning the use of screwdrivers, the one which is INCORRECT is:

   A. Always use a screwdriver with a blade that fits the screw to be turned
   B. Hold the work in one hand while turning the screwdriver with the other
   C. A screwdriver with an insulated handle should be used for making electrical repairs
   D. A screwdriver should not be used as a chisel or hammer

32. A miter box is usually used for

   A. making diagonal cuts
   B. holding the flux in soldering
   C. storing small machine screws
   D. storing precision tools

Questions 33-38.

DIRECTIONS: Questions 33 through 38, inclusive, should be answered in accordance with the following paragraph.

It is important that traffic signals be regularly and effectively maintained. Signals with impaired efficiency cannot be expected to command desired respect. Poorly maintained traffic signs create disrespect in the minds of those who are to obey them and thereby reduce the effectiveness and authority of the signs. Maintenance should receive paramount consideration in the design and purchase of traffic signal equipment. The initial step in a good maintenance program for traffic signals is the establishment of a maintenance record. This record should show the cost of operation and maintenance of different types of equipment. It should give complete information regarding signal operations and indicate where defective planning exists in maintenance programs.

33. The word *effectively*, as used in the above paragraph means MOST NEARLY

   A. occasionally
   B. properly
   C. expensively
   D. cheaply

34. The word *impaired,* as used in the above paragraph, means MOST NEARLY 34.____
    A. reduced   B. increased   C. constant   D. high

35. The word *desired,* as used in the above paragraph, means MOST NEARLY 35.____
    A. public   B. complete   C. wanted   D. enough

36. The word *paramount,* as used in the above paragraph, means MOST NEARLY 36.____
    A. little   B. chief   C. excessive   D. some

37. The word *initial,* as used in the above paragraph, means MOST NEARLY 37.____
    A. first
    C. determining
    B. final
    D. most important

38. The word *defective,* as used in the above paragraph, means MOST NEARLY 38.____
    A. suitable   B. real   C. good   D. faulty

39. A half round file is usually used for 39.____
    A. removing stock rapidly
    B. clearing out square corners
    C. finishing the bottoms of narrow slots
    D. finishing concave surfaces

40. For finishing flat metal surfaces, the type of file usually used is the _____ file. 40.____
    A. pillar   B. hand   C. square   D. drill

KEY (CORRECT ANSWERS)

1. A	11. B	21. A	31. B
2. D	12. A	22. C	32. A
3. A	13. D	23. B	33. B
4. B	14. B	24. C	34. A
5. B	15. A	25. C	35. C
6. C	16. C	26. B	36. B
7. A	17. B	27. C	37. A
8. B	18. B	28. B	38. D
9. D	19. C	29. D	39. D
10. D	20. D	30. B	40. B

TEST 2

DIRECTIONS: Each question or incomplete statement is followed by several suggested answers or completions. Select the one that BEST answers the question or completes the statement. *PRINT THE LETTER OF THE CORRECT ANSWER IN THE SPACE AT THE RIGHT.*

1. The type of pliers usually used for holding or bending thin flat iron stock is known as   1._____

    A. diagonal pliers
    B. round nose pliers
    C. nippers
    D. side cutting pliers

2. An auger bit is usually used for boring a hole in   2._____

    A. brass   B. concrete   C. wood   D. steel

3. The dimension 45" expressed in feet is MOST NEARLY   3._____

    A. 3 1/3   B. 3 1/2   C. 3 3/4   D. 3 7/8

4. The type of hand saw that is used to cut wood along the grain is generally known as a _____ saw.   4._____

    A. band   B. rip   C. back   D. cross cut

5. The LEAST likely cause for the breaking of hacksaw blades is   5._____

    A. using a fine-toothed blade on thin work
    B. using a coarse-toothed blade on thin work
    C. working with a blade that is tightly drawn in the hacksaw frame
    D. applying too much pressure on the work

6. A 1:3:5 mixture of concrete generally refers to a mixture of 1 part of _____, 3 parts of _____, 5 parts of _____.   6._____

    A. gravel, sand, cement
    B. sand, cement, gravel
    C. water, cement, gravel
    D. cement, sand, gravel

7. 85 percent of $5,250 is MOST NEARLY   7._____

    A. $3,463.50   B. $4,361.50   C. $4,462.50   D. $4,666.50

8. A scriber is usually used for   8._____

    A. starting a hole in iron
    B. measuring lengths
    C. cleaning threads
    D. layout work

9. The gauge of an iron sheet indicates its   9._____

    A. thickness
    B. length
    C. weight per square inch
    D. width

10. The type of gears used on the ends of two intersecting shafts 90° to each other for transmitting motion are known as   10._____

    A. spur   B. bevel   C. spline   D. spiral

7

11. If the shortest distance between the edges of two holes drilled in a flat steel plate is 1 1/2" and the diameters of the holes are 3/4" and 1", the distance between centers is MOST NEARLY

    A. 2 1/8"   B. 2 1/4"   C. 2 3/8"   D. 2 3/4"

12. A flat head screw that is identified as a 1/4X 20 - 1" long screw is MOST likely a _____ screw.

    A. wood
    B. sheet metal
    C. cap
    D. machine

13. If your foreman informs you that a traffic signal was obliterated, he MOST likely means that the traffic signal was

    A. stolen   B. obsolete   C. loose   D. destroyed

14. Of the following statements, the one which is MOST correct concerning a *regulatory* traffic sign is that the sign

    A. if disregarded by the driver, is punishable as a misdemeanor
    B. calls attention to conditions that are potentially hazardous to traffic
    C. shows route designations and directions
    D. shows points of interest and other geographical information

15. The MAIN reason for the alternate-side-of-the-street parking regulations is to

    A. facilitate the cleaning of streets
    B. allow room for moving traffic
    C. allow room for delivery trucks
    D. provide space for children to play

16. The geometrical shape of *STOP* signs if

    A. octagonal
    B. triangular
    C. diamond
    D. rectangular

17. In an engine, the MAIN purpose for using oil as a lubricant is to keep

    A. the engine parts from rusting
    B. a film between the moving parts
    C. the internal parts clean, by flushing them
    D. the vibration down

18. The QUICKEST method of determining a defective spark plug is to

    A. take out the spark plugs and examine them
    B. drive to the garage and let a mechanic tell you
    C. short circuit the spark plugs one at a time with an insulated screwdriver
    D. replace all the spark plugs with new ones

19. The device that controls the charging rate of a generator in the generator-battery circuit of an automotive engine is usually the

    A. ignition coil
    B. generator regulator
    C. condenser
    D. generator solenoid

20. The device used with a gasoline engine to change the liquid fuel into vapor and mix it with air is called a(n)

    A. fuel pump
    B. automatic choke
    C. carburetor
    D. vapor regulator

21. The gap between the electrodes of a spark plug is usually measured with a

    A. feeler gauge
    B. flat stock
    C. depth gauge
    D. caliper

22. The proper spark plug gap for MOST truck engines is approximately

    A. .015"   B. .018"   C. .030"   D. .042"

23. A truck mounted air compressor that supplies air to a number of pneumatic tools is usually set to deliver air at APPROXIMATELY _____ psi.

    A. 30   B. 50   C. 90   D. 160

Questions 24-25.

DIRECTIONS: Questions 24 and 25 refer to the sketch below depicting a street intersection.

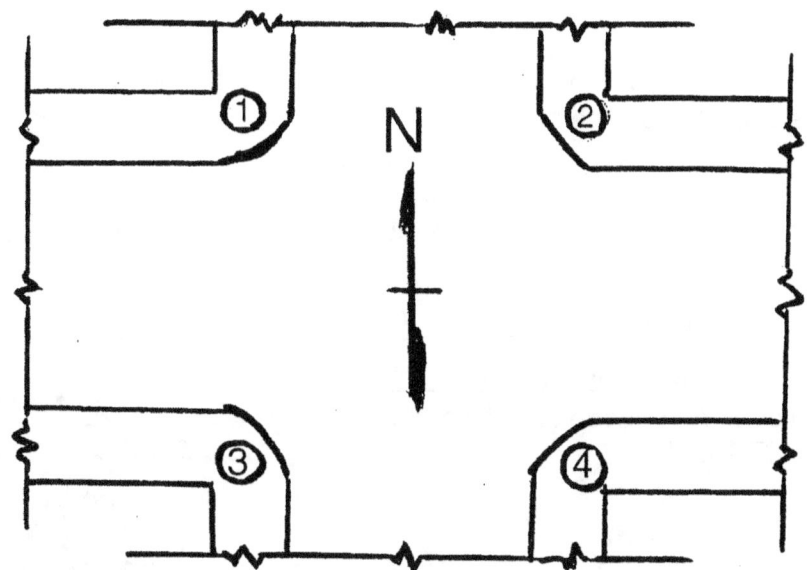

24. In the above sketch, the southeast corner is numbered

    A. 1   B. 2   C. 3   D. 4

25. In the above sketch, the northwest corner is numbered

    A. 1   B. 2   C. 3   D. 4

26. The proper position to place yourself when lifting a heavy box from the floor is to

    A. squat down, bend knees, keep back straight and lift
    B. bend down, hunch back, and lift

C. keep feet away from object, bend back, and lift
D. bend, and use the back muscles when lifting

Questions 27-28.

DIRECTIONS: Questions 27 and 28 refer to the sketches immediately below.

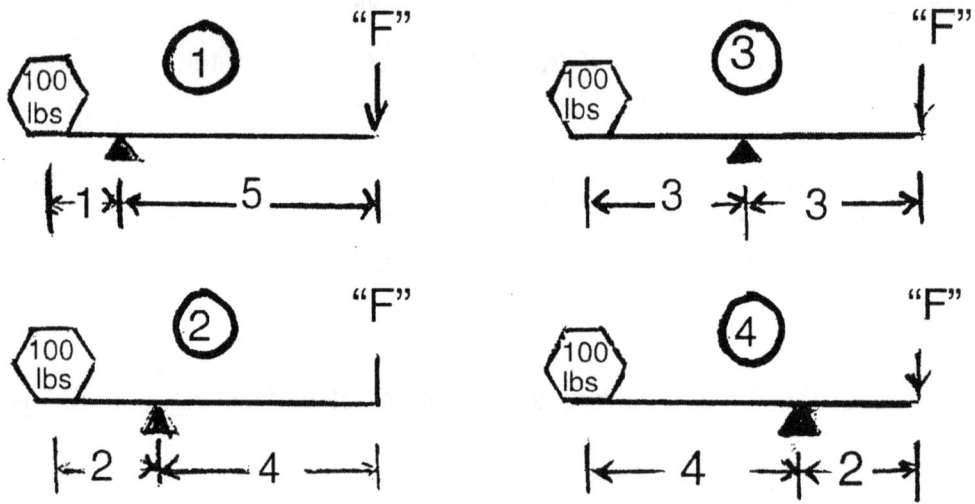

27. The one of the above sketches in which the LEAST force F that is necessary to raise the 100 lb. weight is shown in sketch number 27._____

    A. 1   B. 2   C. 3   D. 4

28. The one of the above sketches in which the MOST force F that is necessary to raise the 100 lb. weight is shown in sketch number 28._____

    A. 1   B. 2   C. 3   D. 4

29. In the sketch shown at the right, the SMALLEST or LEAST pull P in pounds required to hoist a load of 1 1/2 tons is MOST NEARLY 29._____
    A. 500
    B. 1,000
    C. 1,500
    D. 2,000

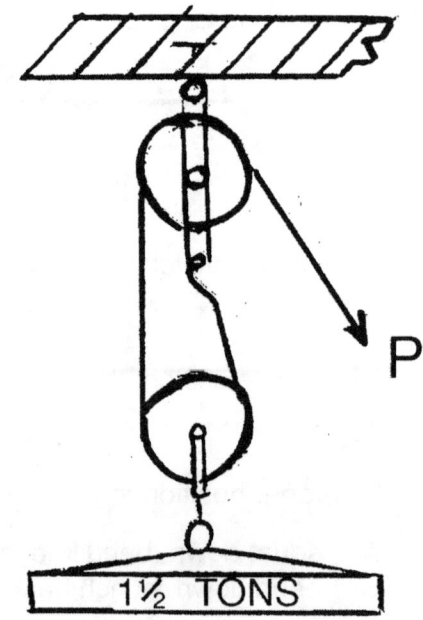

30. Of the following statements, the one which is INCORRECT is: Fibre rope   30._____

    A. should be stored in an air-tight container
    B. should never be stored on the ground
    C. is approximately 10% stronger when wet
    D. should be inspected periodically

31. The term *mousing*, as used in rigging, means MOST NEARLY   31._____

    A. temporarily attaching a rope to a hook
    B. attaching a rope to a tackle block
    C. securing a grip on a rope under strain
    D. placing rope yarn on a hook to prevent load from becoming detached

32. The safe distance that the bottom of a ladder, the top of which is placed against a wall or   32._____
    pole must extend out from the base of the wall or pole, is usually _____ the length of the
    ladder.

    A. 1/2   B. 1/4   C. 1/6   D. 1/8

33. Of the following painting materials, the one which should NOT be used to treat or cover   33._____
    wood ladders is

    A. linseed oil   B. oil paint
    C. shellac   D. varnish

34. A knot that has a non-slipping eye, will not jam, and is easily untied is generally known as   34._____
    a(n)

    A. sheet bend   B. granny
    C. bowline   D. overhand knot

35. A sheepshank knot is PRINCIPALLY used for   35._____

    A. shortening a rope without cutting it
    B. fastening a rope at right angles to a post
    C. attaching a rope to a ring
    D. joining large hawsers

36. Of the following procedures for softening a piece of steel, good practice is to FIRST heat   36._____
    the steel and then

    A. cool it rapidly
    B. dip it in cold water
    C. cool it slowly
    D. cool it in a cold solution of salt

37. Of the following types of measuring rules, the one which can BEST be used to measure   37._____
    directly the circumference of a 4-inch diameter pipe is the _____ rule.

    A. zig-zag   B. folding
    C. caliper   D. push-pull

38. The painting of traffic safety lines and pedestrian crosswalks at busy intersections is one of the jobs of a traffic device maintainer.
The work crew usually protects itself from traffic by

    A. re-routing the traffic at the next intersection
    B. lengthening the time for the *Stop* signal on the traffic light
    C. wearing bright yellow work clothes
    D. placing safety cones to divert traffic away from the work area

39. An unloader is a device that is usually found on a(n)

    A. pneumatic tool
    B. air compressor
    C. storage tank
    D. block and fall

40. A device that can be used repeatedly for marking out shapes on materials is generally called a

    A. blueprint   B. tracing   C. scantling   D. template

KEY (CORRECT ANSWERS)

1. D	11. C	21. A	31. D
2. C	12. D	22. C	32. B
3. C	13. D	23. C	33. B
4. B	14. A	24. D	34. C
5. A	15. A	25. A	35. A
6. D	16. A	26. A	36. C
7. C	17. B	27. A	37. D
8. D	18. C	28. D	38. D
9. A	19. B	29. C	39. B
10. B	20. C	30. A	40. D

EXAMINATION SECTION
TEST 1

DIRECTIONS: Each question or incomplete statement is followed by several suggested answers or completions. Select the one that BEST answers the question or completes the statement. *PRINT THE LETTER OF THE CORRECT ANSWER IN THE SPACE AT THE RIGHT.*

1. When making a preliminary inspection of a new street marking job, the FIRST thing to check is whether

    A. the location is correct
    B. all dimensions are correct
    C. the right paint is specified
    D. traffic can easily be controlled

    1._____

2. After a preliminary inspection of a new street marking job has been made and it has been found that it can be laid out exactly as shown in the drawings received from Plans and Surveys, the site should be reinspected on the first day of actual work to check that

    A. the dimensions are correct according to the plans
    B. the orientation has not changed
    C. excavation work that did not exist on his first inspection does not obstruct his work
    D. the traffic can easily be controlled

    2._____

3. Of the following, it is MOST important when inspecting the installation of a sign in a garage or on a street to check for the _____ the sign.

    A. correct width of
    B. correct area of
    C. correct mounting height of
    D. removal of all scuff marks below

    3._____

4. When inspecting a job site in an off-street parking garage prior to starting a new job involving markings, the FIRST thing to look for is

    A. obstructions such as beams which will require that the layout be altered
    B. oil on the floor
    C. paint splashes on the floor
    D. vehicles which must be moved

    4._____

5. The one of the following items which should be checked on a job involving the installation of custom-made highway guide signs but which need NOT be checked during the installation of street regulatory signs is the _____ of the sign.

    A. color
    B. wording and spelling
    C. width
    D. area

    5._____

6. Assume that you are facing east while standing on the northwest corner of the intersection of two streets. One of these streets runs north and south, and the other runs east and west.
The SOUTHWEST corner of this intersection is

    6._____

13

A. *directly* across the street in front of you
B. *directly* across the street to your right
C. *diagonally* across the intersection from you
D. *directly* across the street to your left

7. A street running north and south intersects a street running east and west. Four men designated as A, B, C, and D are each on a different corner of the intersection. A is on the NW corner and faces east; B is on the SW corner and faces north; C is on the SE corner and faces west; and D is on the NE corner and faces west.
The two men who are facing DIRECTLY toward each other are

A. A and B B. B and C C. C and D D. A and D

8. Of the following, the MOST important item to check during a routine inspection of an air compressor is the

A. amount of air used daily
B. number of hours it has been operated
C. diaphragm diameter
D. condition of the paint finish

9. Assume that a crew assigned to you goes out to paint some street markings on a street which has a great deal of traffic.
The traffic should be diverted away from the working area by means of

A. Class I barricades
B. Class II barricades
C. Class I barricades and cones
D. cones

10. Assume that an extensive area within an off-street parking facility has caved in. Until repairs are completed, cars should be kept away from this area by means of

A. Class I barricades
B. Class I barricades and flasher lights
C. Class II barricades and cones
D. warning signs and Class I barricades

11. A line of traffic cones, being used to divert traffic fron men painting cross-walks in the lane nearest the curb, should begin at the curb at a point whose distance fron the working area is _____ feet, and the cones should be _____ feet apart.

A. 40; 10 B. 60; 15 C. 80; 15 D. 100; 10

12. Crews doing street marking work at night should wear

A. gray coveralls and set out traffic cones to divert traffic away from the area
B. reflectorized vests and set out traffic cones to divert traffic away from the area
C. bright yellow helmets and gray coveralls
D. bright blue helmets and set out traffic cones to divert traffic away from the area

13. Assume that the top of a 12 foot ladder is to be placed against a wall. The RECOMMENDED safe practice is that the ladder should be placed so that the distance from the bottom of the ladder to the base of the wall is _____ ft.

    A. 1   B. 2   C. 3   D. 5

14. According to the State Vehicle and Traffic Law, when driving at a speed of 40 miles per hour along a dry road, the driver should maintain a distance between his car and the car immediately ahead of him of AT LEAST _____ car lengths.

    A. 2   B. 3   C. 4   D. 5

15. Assume that a man has been knocked unconscious.
    Which of the following should NOT be done to the victim?

    A. Give him something to drink
    B. Hold a handkerchief with spirits of ammonia under his nose if he is breathing
    C. Keep him covered with a blanket
    D. Give him artificial respiration if he is not breathing

16. A paint sprayer may have gauges showing the pressure of the tank, the paint pressure, and the atomizer pressure. When the sprayer is operating properly, the

    A. paint pressure is higher than the tank pressure
    B. atomizer pressure is higher than the tank pressure
    C. paint and atomizer pressures are equal
    D. atomizer pressure is higher than the paint pressure

17. A certain paint can cover 310 square feet per gallon. The number of gallons of this paint required to paint 200 lines each 6 inches wide and 18 feet-6 inches long is MOST NEARLY

    A. 2   B. 4   C. 6   D. 8

18. Paint brushes that are used with an oil-based paint are USUALLY cleaned with

    A. turpentine   B. linseed oil
    C. acetone   D. alcohol

19. The air in an air compressor cylinder is DIRECTLY compressed by the

    A. pressure switch   B. surge chamber
    C. cam   D. piston

20. The part which permits the motor of an air compressor to start free of load regardless of the tank pressure is the

    A. unloader valve   B. surge tank
    C. pressure switch   D. drain cock

21. Assume that instead of spraying paint properly, a paint sprayer ejects a solid stream of paint from its nozzle. The one of the following that may cause this condition is

    A. compressor tank pressure is too high
    B. compressor tank pressure is lower than the atomizer pressure
    C. atomizer pressure is higher than the paint pressure
    D. atomizer pressure is too low

22. The one of the following which is a *regulatory* sign is the

    A. bump sign B. low clearance sign
    C. route marker D. stop sign

23. The one of the following which is a *regulatory* sign is the _____ sign.

    A. yield B. stop ahead
    C. side road D. slippery when wet

24. The one of the following signs which is octagonal is the _____ sign.

    A. speed limit B. stop ahead
    C. road narrows D. stop

25. Of the following statements, the one which gives the function of a *warning* sign is that this sign

    A. indicates route designations, destinations, or distances
    B. gives the driver notice of laws or regulations that apply at a given place, disregard of which is punishable as a violation or a misdemeanor
    C. calls attention to conditions in or adjacent to a street that are potentially hazardous to traffic
    D. indicates points of interest or geographical locations

26. The regulation manual on temporary traffic control of the department of traffic defines Class II barricades as being of the *horse* type with only one rail.
    It further specifies that the rail should be marked on

    A. *one* side with 3" vertical red and white, black and white, or black and yellow reflectorized stripes
    B. *both* sides with 3" vertical red and white, black and white, or black and yellow stripes
    C. *both* sides with 6" reflectorized red and white, black and white, or black and yellow stripes sloping at an angle of 45
    D. *both* sides with 6" vertical red and white or black and white stripes

27. Silk screening is a method of

    A. temporarily concealing signs already erected but not ready to be used
    B. painting signs
    C. protecting newly painted crosswalks until they dry
    D. protecting reflectorized signs from dust

28. The blade of a snow plow is USUALLY made of

    A. monel B. steel
    C. tungsten carbide D. beryllium

29. To PROPERLY check the lifting device of a snow plow at the beginning of the snow season, the plow blade should be

    A. raised and kept in that position for at least three minutes in order to detect leaks in the system
    B. raised by the lifting device once to see if it operates

C. dropped quickly after being brought to the raised position
D. raised and lowered and then the operation should be repeated

30. At the present time, the department of traffic USUALLY reflectorizes signs by

   A. coating the portion of the sign to be reflectorized with very tiny glass beads held by an adhesive base
   B. outlining the reflectorized portion of the sign with large glass *bull's eyes*
   C. making the reflectorized portion of the sign with *Scotch Lite*
   D. painting the reflectorized portion of the sign with *Luminar*

KEY (CORRECT ANSWERS)

1. A	11. D	21. D
2. C	12. B	22. D
3. C	13. C	23. A
4. A	14. C	24. D
5. B	15. A	25. C
6. B	16. D	26. C
7. D	17. C	27. B
8. B	18. A	28. B
9. D	19. D	29. A
10. C	20. A	30. C

TEST 2

DIRECTIONS: Each question or incomplete statement is followed by several suggested answers or completions. Select the one that BEST answers the question or completes the statement. *PRINT THE LETTER OF THE CORRECT ANSWER IN THE SPACE AT THE RIGHT.*

1. The material which causes the hydraulic plunger of a heavy duty hydraulic jack to move is
   A. oil   b. petrolatum   C. alcohol   D. glycerol

   1.____

2. "Vapor Lock" will DIRECTLY affect the operation of
   A. air compressors
   B. pneumatic hammers
   C. paint sprayers
   D. automobiles

   2.____

3. Of the following grades of SAE crankcase oils, the one which is RECOMMENDED for year-round use is
   A. 10W-30   B. 30   C. 20W   D. 10W

   3.____

4. Of the following, wheel misalignment in an automobile USUALLY results in
   A. frequent stalling
   B. improper clutch action
   C. rapid tire wear
   D. impaired shock absorber action

   4.____

5. Of the following, the EASIEST method of locating a defective spark plug in a gasoline engine is to
   A. take out all the spark plugs and examine them
   B. short circuit the spark plugs one at a time
   C. replace all of the spark plugs with new ones
   D. rotate all the spark plugs

   5.____

6. The one of the following conditions which may cause the fuel mixture in a gasoline engine to be too rich is
   A. water in the gasoline
   B. a dirty air cleaner
   C. a punctured muffler
   D. vapor lock in the fuel line

   6.____

7. If the battery of a car is constantly running dry, the one of the following items which should be checked FIRST is the
   A. generator
   B. ignition switch
   C. relay
   D. voltage regulator

   7.____

8. In a gasoline engine, the throttle vale is a part of the
   A. fuel tank
   B. carbureto
   C. crankcase
   D. water radiator

   8.____

9. If a car does not start on damp days, the trouble is MOST likely in the _____ system.
   A. ignition   B. fuel   C. lubricating   D. cooling

10. The one of the following terms that applies to the relationship between the front axle and the steering mechanism of an automobile is
    A. camber   B. armature   C. crankshaft   D. camshaft

11. The function of a carburetor on a gasoline engine is to
    A. filter the gasoline
    B. mix air and gasoline in the correct proportions
    C. pump the gasoline into the cylinder
    D. filter the air coming into the engine

12. An automotive ignition coil is used in the electrical system of a gasoline engine to
    A. reduce arcing across the breaker points
    B. transformers low voltage to high voltage
    C. operate the ignition switch
    D. charge the battery

13. The purpose of the thermostat in the cooling system of a gasoline engine is to
    A. indicate the temperature of the cooling water
    B. control water flow so as to prevent excessive pressure in the radiator
    C. prevent overheating of the cooling water
    D. prevent circulation of the cooling water when the engine is cold

14. Of the following sets of items, the BEST one to use to clean and adjust ignition points is
    A. crescent wrench, V-block, and sandpaper
    B. screwdriver, feeler gauge, and point file
    C. scraper, micrometer, and sandpaper
    D. pincers, micrometer, and emery cloth

15. The MAIN reason for not allowing oily rags to accumulate in storage closets is that
    A. a rancid odor will develop near the closet
    B. the closet will look messy
    C. oil will drip onto the floor
    D. a fire may start by spontaneous combustion

16. A certain paint can cover 310 square feet per gallon. The number of gallons of this paint required to paint 200 lines each 6 inches wide and 18 feet, 6 inches long is MOST nearly
    A. 2   B. 4   C. 6   D. 8

17. Paint brushes that are used with an oil-based paint are usually cleaned with
    A. turpentine   B. linseed oil   C. acetone   D. alcohol

18. Assume that, while you are using an electric drill with a long electric cord, the drill suddenly stops operating. Of the following, the FIRST thing that you should do is to
    A. remove the casing of the drill to see whether the insulation of the armature is damaged
    B. check whether the cord is still plugged into the outlet
    C. check the fuses in the supply circuit
    D. inspecft the cord for a broken wire

18.____

19. A cold chisel with a "mushroomed" head is properly "dressed" by
    A. filing the cutting edge
    B. heating the head until it is red hot and quenching it in oil
    C. grinding off the turned over material
    D. heating the head of the chisel until it is red hot and, after letting it cool slowly, tapping it until all the chips fall off

19.____

20. Of the following sets of items, the BEST one to use to clean and adjust ignition points is
    A. crescent wrench, V-block, and sandpaper
    B. screwdriver, feeler gauge, and point file
    C. scraper, micrometer, and sandpaper
    D. pincers, micrometer, and emery cloth

20.____

KEY (CORRECT ANSWERS)

1.	A	11.	B
2.	D	12.	B
3.	A	13.	D
4.	C	14.	B
5.	B	15.	D
6.	B	16.	C
7.	D	17.	A
8.	B	18.	B
9.	A	19.	C
10.	A	20.	B

TEST 3

DIRECTIONS: Each question or incomplete statement is followed by several suggested answers or completions. Select the one that BEST answers the question or completes the statement. *PRINT THE LETTER OF THE CORRECT ANSWER IN THE SPACE AT THE RIGHT.*

1. Assume that, while you are using an electric drill with a long electric cord, the drill suddenly stops operating. Of the following, the FIRST thing that you should do is to
   A. remove the casing of the drill to see whether the insulation of the armature is damaged
   B. check whether the cord is still plugged into the outlet
   C. check the fuses in the supply circuit
   D. inspect the cord for a broken wire

   1.____

2. A cold chisel with a "mushroomed" head is PROPERLY "dressed" by
   A. filing the cutting edge
   B. heating the head until it is red hot and quenching it in oil
   C. grinding off the turned over material
   D. heating the head of the chisel until it is red hot and, after letting it cool slowly, tapping it until all the chips fall off

   2.____

3. A pipe reamer is used to
   A. thread pipe
   B. enlarge the size of a pipe
   C. remove burrs from the inside of a pipe
   D. join pipes of different sizes

   3.____

4. Where only a short swing of the handle is possible, the BEST tool to use to tighten a nut or bolt is the _____ wrench.
   A. Stillson   B. open end   C. monkey   D. ratchet

   4.____

5. The wrench which is used on set screws is COMMONLY called the _____ wrench.
   A. torque   B. Allen   C. Stillson   D. Crescent

   5.____

6. A box wrench is BEST used on
   A. Allen screws
   C. hexagonal nuts
   B. pipe fittings
   D. knurled thumb screws

   6.____

7. The BEST screwdriver to use when driving screws in close quarters is the
   A. butt   B. angled   C. Phillips   D. offset

   7.____

8. A "12-24" screw is MOST likely a _____ screw.
   A. machine   b. sheet metal   C. lag   D. wood

   8.____

21

9. The one of the following fasteners which is threaded at both ends is the
   A. lag screw	B. stud
   C. bolt	D. machine screw

10. Tips of masonry drills are USUALLY made of
    A. carbide	B. corundum	C. mild steel	D. beryllium

11. A 5-inch length of pipe with male threads at each end is called a
    A. stud	B. coupling	C. sleeve	D. nipple

12. Grade No. 2 sandpaper is
    A. finer than grade 1/0	B. coarser than grade 3
    C. finer than grade 2/0	D. coarser than grade 1

13. The one of the following lists of materials which includes ALL of the ingredients of concrete is cement,
    A. gravel, and water	B. lime, sand, and water
    C. sand, gravel, and water	D. sand, and water

14. The MAIN purpose of the tool known as a file card is to _____ files.
    A. clean	B. sort out
    C. prevent damage to	D. sharpen

15. The pull exerted by a man lifting a 200 lb. load by means of a four-part block and fall, ignoring friction, is _____ lbs.
    A. 100	B. 75	C. 50	D. 25

16. Of the following, turpentine is a solvent for
    A. shellac	B. latex paint
    C. calcimine	D. red lead paint

17. In a truck's gasoline engine, the condenser is a part of the
    A. distributor	B. cooling system
    C. power take off	D. fuel system

18. Pneumatic tools are operated by a(n)
    A. air compressor	B. Pelton wheel
    C. Archimedean screw	D. hydraulic ram

19. The gauge on the tank of an air compressor measures
    A. temperature of air in the tank	B. pressure of air in the tank
    C. humidity of the atmosphere	D. barometric pressure

20. A paint sprayer may have gauges showing the pressure of the tank, the paint pressure, and the atomizer pressure. When the sprayer is operating properly, the

20.____

    A. paint pressure is higher than the tank pressure
    B. atomizer pressure is higher than the tank pressure
    C. paint and atomizer pressures are equal
    D. atomizer pressure is higher than the paint pressure

KEY (CORRECT ANSWERS)

1.	B	11.	D
2.	C	12.	D
3.	C	13.	C
4.	D	14.	A
5.	B	15.	C
6.	C	16.	D
7.	D	17.	A
8.	A	18.	A
9.	B	19.	B
10.	A	20.	D

EXAMINATION SECTION
TEST 1

DIRECTIONS: Each question or incomplete statement is followed by several suggested answers or completions. Select the one that BEST answers the question or completes the statement. *PRINT THE LETTER OF THE CORRECT ANSWER IN THE SPACE AT THE RIGHT.*

1. A bit is held in a hand drill by means of a(n)

    A. arbor B. chuck C. collet D. clamp

2. The type of screw that MOST often requires a countersunk hole is a _____ head.

    A. flat B. round C. fillister D. hexagon

3. Instead of using the ordinary 1 piece screwdriver, a screwdriver bit is MOST often used with a brace because of the

    A. increased length of the brace
    B. different types of bits available
    C. increased leverage of the brace
    D. ability to work in tight corners

4. A thread gage is usually used to measure the

    A. thickness of a thread
    B. diameter of a thread
    C. number of threads per inch
    D. height of a thread

5. The wheel of a glass cutter is BEST lubricated with

    A. kerosene
    B. linseed oil
    C. varnolene
    D. diesel oil

6. A nail set is a

    A. group of nails of the same size and type
    B. group of nails of different sizes but the same type
    C. tool used to extract nails
    D. tool used to drive nails below the surface of wood

7. To test for leaks in a gas line, it is BEST to use

    A. a match
    B. soapy water
    C. a colored dye
    D. ammonia

8. Routing is the process of cutting a

    A. strip out of sheet metal
    B. groove in wood
    C. chamfer on a shaft
    D. core out of concrete

9. A hacksaw frame has a wing nut mainly to

    A. make it easier to replace blades
    B. increase the strength of the frame
    C. prevent vibration of the blade
    D. adjust the length of the frame

10. A mitre box is usually used with a _____ saw.
    A. hack   B. crosscut   C. rip   D. back

11. A continuous flexible saw blade is MOST often used on a _____ saw.
    A. radial   B. band   C. swing   D. table

12. A pipe reamer is used to
    A. clean out a length of pipe
    B. thread pipe
    C. remove burrs from the ends of pipe
    D. seal pipe joints

13. To lay out a straight cut on a piece of wood at the same angle as the cut on a second piece of wood, the PROPER tool to use is a
    A. bevel   B. cope   C. butt gauge   D. clevis

14. Before drilling a hole in a piece of metal, an indentation should be made with a _____ punch.
    A. pin   B. taper   C. center   D. drift

15. Curved cuts in wood are BEST made with a _____ saw.
    A. jig   B. veneer   C. radial   D. swing

16. A face plate is generally used to
    A. hold material while working with it on a lathe
    B. smooth out irregularities in a metal plate
    C. protect the finish on a metal plate
    D. locate centers of holes to be drilled on a drill press

17. A die would be used to
    A. gage the groove in a splined shaft
    B. cut a thread on a metal rod
    C. hold a piece to be machined on a milling machine
    D. control the depth of a hole to be drilled in a piece of metal

18. Before using a ladle to scoop up molten solder, you should make sure that the ladle is dry.
    This is done to prevent
    A. the solder from sticking to the ladle
    B. impurities from getting into the solder
    C. injuries due to splashing solder
    D. cooling of the solder

19. To PROPERLY adjust the gap on a spark plug, you should use a(n) 19._____
    A. inside caliper   B. center gauge
    C. wire type feeler gauge   D. micrometer

20. The length of the MOST common type of folding wood rule is _____ feet. 20._____
    A. 4   B. 5   C. 6   D. 7

21. A four-foot mason's level is usually used to determine whether the top of a wall is level and whether it is 21._____
    A. square   B. plumb   C. rigid   D. in line

22. To match a tongue in a board, the matching board MUST have a 22._____
    A. rabbet   B. chamfer   C. bead   D. groove

23. When driving screws in close quarters, the BEST type of screwdriver to use is a(n) 23._____
    A. Phillips   B. offset   C. butt   D. angled

24. The term 12-24 refers to a _____ screw. 24._____
    A. wood   B. lag
    C. sheet metal   D. machine

25. To measure the length of a curved line on a drawing or plan, the PROPER tool to use in addition to a ruler is(are) 25._____
    A. dividers   B. calipers
    C. surface gage   D. radius gage

26. For the standard machine screw, the diameter of a tap drill is generally 26._____
    A. *equal* to the diameter of the shaft of the screw at the base of the threads (the root diameter)
    B. *larger* than the root diameter, but smaller than the diameter of the screw
    C. *equal* to the diameter of the screw
    D. *larger* than the diameter of the screw

27. In order to drill a 1" hole accurately with a drill press, you should 27._____
    A. drill at high speeds
    B. use very little pressure on the drill
    C. drill partway down, release pressure on the drill, and then continue drilling
    D. drill a pilot hole first

28. Before taking apart an electric motor to repair, punch marks are sometimes placed on the casing near each other. 28._____
    The MOST probable reason for doing this is to
    A. make sure the parts lock together on reassembly
    B. properly line up the parts that are next to each other
    C. keep track of the number of parts in the assembly
    D. identify all the parts as coming from the one motor

29. To locate a point on a floor directly under a point on the ceiling, the PROPER tool to use is a

    A. square
    B. line level
    C. height gage
    D. plumb bob

Question 30.

DIRECTIONS: Question 30 is based on the diagram appearing below.

30. In the above diagram, the full P required to lift the weight a distance of four feet is MOST NEARLY _____ lbs.

    A. 50
    B. 67
    C. 75
    D. 100

31. The EASIEST tool to use to determine whether the edge of a board is at right angles to the face of the board is a

    A. rafter square
    B. try square
    C. protractor
    D. marking gage

32. *Whetting* refers to

    A. tempering of tools by dipping them in water
    B. annealing of tools by heating and slow cooling
    C. brazing of carbide tips on tools
    D. sharpening of tools

33. The MOST difficult part of a plank to plane is the

    A. face
    B. side
    C. end
    D. back

34. To prevent wood from splitting when drilling with an auger, it is BEST to

    A. use even pressure on the bit
    B. drill at a slow speed
    C. hold the wood tightly in a vise
    D. back up the wood with a piece of scrap wood

35. The term *dressing a grinding wheel* refers to 35.____

   A. setting up the wheel on the arbor
   B. restoring the sharpness of a wheel face that has become clogged
   C. placing flanges against the sides of the wheel
   D. bringing the wheel up to speed before using it

36. Heads of rivets are BEST cut off with a 36.____

   A. hacksaw   B. cold chisel
   C. fly cutter   D. reamer

37. A *V-block* is especially useful to 37.____

   A. prevent damage to work held in a vise
   B. hold round stock while a hole is being drilled into it
   C. prevent rolling of round stock stored on the ground
   D. shim up the end of a machine so that it is level

38. A full set of taps for a given size usually consists of a _____ tap. 38.____

   A. taper and bottoming
   B. taper and plug
   C. plug and bottoming
   D. taper, plug, and bottoming

39. Round thread cutting dies are usually held in stock by means of 39.____

   A. wing nuts   B. clamps   C. set screws   D. bolts

40. The one of the following diagrams that shows the plan view and the elevation of a counterbored hole is 40.____

A.

B.

C.

D.

41. With regard to pipe, *I.D.* usually means 41.____

   A. inside diameter   B. inside dressed
   C. invert diameter   D. installation date

42. A compression fitting is MOST often used to

    A. lubricate a wheel
    B. join two pieces of tubing
    C. reduce the diameter of a hole
    D. press fit a gear to a shaft

43. The shape of a mill file is basically

    A. flat   B. half round   C. triangular   D. square

44. Of the following, the ratio of tin to lead that will produce the solder with the LOWEST melting point is

    A. 30-70   B. 40-60   C. 50-50   D. 60-40

45. A safe edge on a file is one that

    A. is smooth and can not cut
    B. has a finer cut than the face of the file
    C. is rounded to prevent scratches
    D. has a coarser cut than the face of the file

46. The MOST frequent use of a file card is to _____ files.

    A. sort out   B. clean
    C. prevent damage to   D. prevent clogging of

47. The BEST way of determining whether a grinding wheel has an internal crack is to

    A. run the wheel at high speed, stop it, and examine the wheel
    B. spray lubricating oil on the sides of the wheel and check the amount of absorption of the oil
    C. hit the wheel with a rubber hammer and listen to the sound
    D. drop the wheel sharply on a table and then check the wheel

48. If a grinding wheel has worn to a smaller diameter, the BEST practice to follow is to

    A. discard the wheel
    B. continue using the wheel as before
    C. use the wheel, but at a faster speed
    D. use the wheel, but at a slower speed

49. With respect to the ordinary awl,

    A. only the tip is hardened
    B. the entire blade is hardened
    C. the tip is tempered, and the rest of the blade is hardened
    D. the entire blade is tempered

50. To prevent overheating of drills, it is BEST to use _____ oil.

    A. cutting   B. lubricating
    C. penetrating   D. heating

KEY (CORRECT ANSWERS)

1. B	11. B	21. B	31. B	41. A
2. A	12. C	22. D	32. D	42. B
3. C	13. A	23. B	33. C	43. A
4. C	14. C	24. D	34. D	44. D
5. A	15. A	25. A	35. B	45. A
6. D	16. A	26. B	36. B	46. B
7. B	17. B	27. D	37. B	47. C
8. B	18. C	28. B	38. D	48. C
9. A	19. C	29. D	39. C	49. A
10. D	20. C	30. D	40. A	50. A

TEST 2

DIRECTIONS: Each question or incomplete statement is followed by several suggested answers or completions. Select the one that BEST answers the question or completes the statement. *PRINT THE LETTER OF THE CORRECT ANSWER IN THE SPACE AT THE RIGHT.*

1. Crocus cloth is commonly used to 1.____

    A. protect finely machined surfaces from damage while the machines are being repaired
    B. remove rust from steel
    C. protect floors and furniture while painting walls
    D. wipe up oil and grease that has spilled

2. Before using a new paint brush, the FIRST operation should be to 2.____

    A. remove loose bristles
    B. soak the brush in linseed oil
    C. hang the brush up overnight
    D. clean the brush with turpentine

3. When sharpening a hand saw, the FIRST operation is to 3.____

    A. file the teeth down to the same height
    B. shape the teeth to the proper profile
    C. bend the teeth over to provide clearance when sawing
    D. clean the gullies with a file

4. To prevent solder from dripping when soldering a vertical seam, it is BEST to 4.____

    A. hold a waxed rag under the soldering iron
    B. use the soldering iron in a horizontal position
    C. tin the soldering iron on one side only
    D. solder the seam in the order from bottom to top

5. If a round nut has two holes in the face, the PROPER type wrench to use to tighten this nut is a(n) 5.____

    A. Stillson   B. monkey   C. spanner   D. open end

6. A box wrench is BEST used on 6.____

    A. pipe fittings   B. flare nuts
    C. hexagonal nuts   D. Allen screws

7. To prevent damage to fine finishes on metal work that is to be held in a vise, you should 7.____

    A. clamp the work lightly
    B. use brass inserts on the vise
    C. wrap the work with cloth before inserting it in the vise
    D. substitute a smooth face plate for the serrated plate on the vise

8. The MOST frequent use for a turnbuckle is to 8.____
   A. tighten a guy wire
   B. adjust shims on a machine
   C. bolt a bracket to a wall
   D. support electric cable from a ceiling

9. To form the head of a tinner's rivet, the PROPER tool to use is a rivet 9.____
   A. anvil   B. plate   C. set   D. brake

10. A socket speed handle MOST closely resembles a 10.____
    A. screwdriver   B. brace   C. spanner   D. spin grip

11. Tips of masonry drills are usually made of 11.____
    A. steel   B. carbide   C. corundum   D. monel

12. The BEST flux to use for soldering galvanized iron is 12.____
    A. resin   B. sal ammoniac
    C. borax   D. muriatic acid

13. The one of the following that is NOT a common type of oilstone is 13.____
    A. silicon carbide   B. aluminum oxide
    C. hard Arkansas   D. pumice

14. A method of joining metals using temperatures intermediate between soldering and welding is 14.____
    A. corbelling   B. brazing   C. annealing   D. lapping

15. When an unusually high degree of accuracy is required with woodwork, lines should be marked with a 15.____
    A. pencil ground to a chisel point
    B. pencil line over a crayon line
    C. sharp knife point
    D. scriber

16. The MOST important difference between pipe threads and V threads on bolts is that pipe threads are usually 16.____
    A. longer   B. sharper
    C. tapered   D. more evenly spaced

17. A street elbow differs from the ordinary elbow in that the street elbow has 17.____
    A. different diameter threads at each end
    B. male threads at one end and female threads at the other
    C. female threads at both ends
    D. male threads at both ends

18. Water hammer in a pipe line can MOST often be stopped by the installation of a(n) 18.____
    A. pressure reducing valve   B. expansion joint
    C. flexible coupling   D. air chamber

19. If water is leaking from the top part of a bibcock, the part that should be replaced is MOST likely the

    A. bibb washer
    B. packing
    C. seat
    D. bibb screw

20. When joining electric wires together in a fixture box, the BEST thing to use are wire

    A. connectors   B. couplings   C. clamps   D. bolts

21. If the name plate of a motor indicates that it is a split phase motor, it is LIKELY that this motor

    A. is a universal motor
    B. operates on DC only
    C. operates on AC only
    D. operates either on DC at full power or on AC at reduced power

22. To make driving of a screw into hard wood easier, it is BEST to lubricate the threads of the screw with

    A. varnoline
    B. penetrating oil
    C. beeswax
    D. cutting oil

23. Assume that a thermostatically controlled oil heater fails to operate. To determine whether it is the thermostat that is at fault, you should

    A. check the circuit breaker
    B. connect a wire across the terminals of the thermostat
    C. replace the contacts on the thermostat
    D. put an ammeter on the line

24. The function of the carburetor on a gasoline engine is to

    A. mix the air and gasoline properly
    B. filter the fuel
    C. filter the air to engine
    D. pump the gasoline into the cylinder

25. If a car owner complains that the battery in his car is constantly running dry, the item that should be checked FIRST is the

    A. fan belt
    B. generator
    C. voltage regulator
    D. relay

26. On MOST modern automobiles, foot brake pressure is transmitted to the brake drums by

    A. air pressure
    B. mechanical linkage
    C. hydraulic fluid
    D. electro-magnetic force

27. Assume that the engine of a car remains cold even though it is run for a period of time. The part that is MOST likely at fault is the

    A. heat by-pass valve
    B. thermostat
    C. heater control
    D. choke

28. To permit easy stripping of concrete forms, they should be 28._____
   A. dried   B. oiled   C. wet down   D. cleaned

29. To prevent honey combing in concrete, the concrete should be 29._____
   A. vibrated
   B. cured
   C. heated in cold weather
   D. protected from the rain

30. The MAIN reason for using wire mesh in connection with concrete work is to 30._____
   A. strain the impurities from the sand
   B. increase the strength of the concrete
   C. hold the forms together
   D. protect the concrete till it hardens

31. Segregation of concrete is MOST often caused by pouring concrete 31._____
   A. in cold weather
   B. from too great a height
   C. too rapidly
   D. into a form in which the concrete has already begun to harden

32. Headers in carpentry are MOST closely associated with 32._____
   A. trimmers
   B. cantilevers
   C. posts
   D. newels

33. Joists are very often supported by 33._____
   A. suspenders
   B. base plates
   C. anchor bolts
   D. bridal irons

34. At outside corners, the type of joint MOST frequently used on a baseboard is the 34._____
   A. plowed
   B. mitered
   C. mortise and tenon
   D. butt

35. The vehicle used with latex paints is usually 35._____
   A. linseed oil
   B. shellac
   C. varnish
   D. water

36. *Boxing* of paint refers to the _____ of paints. 36._____
   A. mixing   B. storage   C. use   D. canning

37. When painting wood, nail holes should be puttied 37._____
   A. *before* applying the prime coat
   B. *after* applying the prime coat but before the second coat
   C. *after* applying the second coat but before the third coat
   D. *after* applying the third coat

38. In laying up a brick wall, you find that at the end of the wall there is not enough space for a full brick. 38._____
   You should use a

   A. stretcher   B. bat   C. corbel   D. bull nose

39. Pointing a brick wall is the same as

   A. truing up the wall
   B. topping the wall with a waterproof surface
   C. repairing the mortar joints in the wall
   D. providing a foundation for the wall

40. The pigment MOST often used in a prime coat of paint on steel to prevent rusting is

   A. lampblack   B. calcimine
   C. zinc oxide   D. red lead

41. If you find a co-worker lying unconscious across an electric wire, the FIRST thing you should do is

   A. get him off the wire   B. call the foreman
   C. get a doctor   D. shut off the power

42.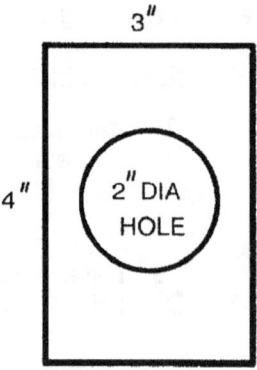

   The area of the metal plate shown above, minus the hole area, is MOST NEARLY _____ square inches.

   A. 8.5   B. 8.9   C. 9.4   D. 10.1

43.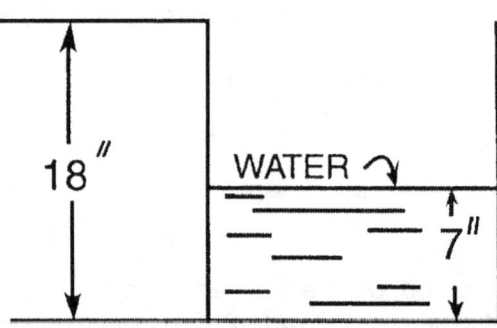

   The percentage of the above tank that is filled with water is MOST NEARLY

   A. 33   B. 35   C. 37   D. 39

44.

 TOP VIEW

 FRONT VIEW

The top and front view of an object are shown above. The right side view will MOST likely look like

A. 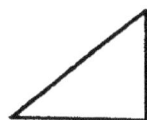   B.    C.    D.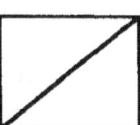

45.

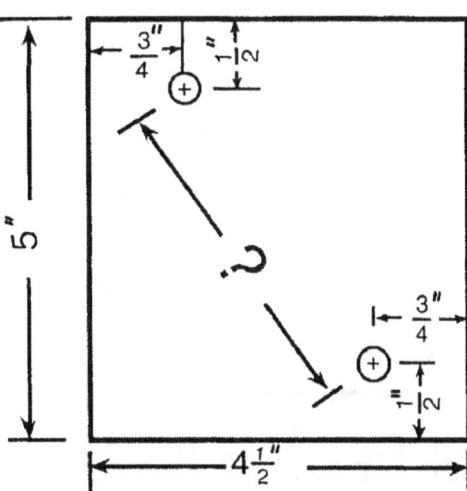

The distance between centers of the holes in the above diagram is MOST NEARLY

A. $4\frac{1}{2}"$ B. 4 3/4"   C. 5"   D. $5\frac{1}{4}"$

Questions 46-48.

DIRECTIONS: Questions 46 through 48, inclusive, are to be answered in accordance with the paragraph below.

A steam heating system with steam having a pressure of less than 10 pounds is called a low-pressure system. The majority of steam-heating systems are of this type. The steam may be provided by low-pressure boilers installed expressly for the purpose, or it may be gener-

ated in boilers at a higher pressure and reduced in pressure before admitted to the heating mains. In other instances, it may be possible to use exhaust steam which has been made to run engines and other machines and which still contains enough heat to be utilized in the heating system. The first case represents the system of heating used in the ordinary residence or other small building; the other two represent the systems of heating employed in industrial buildings where a power plant is installed for general power purposes.

46. According to the above paragraph, whether or not a steam heating system is considered a low pressure system is determined by the pressure

    A. generated by the boiler
    B. in the heating main
    C. at the inlet side of the reducing valve
    D. of the exhaust

47. According to the above paragraph, steam used for heating is sometimes obtained from steam

    A. generated principally to operate machinery
    B. exhausted from larger boilers
    C. generated at low pressure and brought up to high pressure before being used
    D. generated by engines other than boilers

48. As used in the above paragraph, the word *expressly* means

    A. rapidly   B. specifically
    C. usually   D. mainly

49. Of the following words, the one that is CORRECTLY spelled is

    A. suficient   B. sufficant
    C. sufficient   D. suficant

50. Of the following words, the one that is CORRECTLY spelled is

    A. fairly   B. fairley   C. farely   D. fairlie

KEY (CORRECT ANSWERS)

1. B	11. B	21. C	31. B	41. D
2. A	12. D	22. C	32. A	42. B
3. A	13. D	23. B	33. D	43. D
4. C	14. B	24. A	34. B	44. A
5. C	15. C	25. C	35. D	45. C
6. C	16. C	26. C	36. A	46. B
7. B	17. B	27. B	37. B	47. A
8. A	18. D	28. B	38. B	48. B
9. C	19. B	29. A	39. C	49. C
10. B	20. A	30. B	40. D	50. A

EXAMINATION SECTION
TEST 1

DIRECTIONS: Each question or incomplete statement is followed by several suggested answers or completions. Select the one that BEST answers the question or completes the statement. *PRINT THE LETTER OF THE CORRECT ANSWER IN THE SPACE AT THE RIGHT.*

1. The composition of plumber's solder for wiping is APPROXIMATELY (ratio of tin to lead)   1._____

    A. 40-60   B. 50-50   C. 60-40   D. 70-30

2. A device used to lift sewage to the level of a sewer from a floor below the sewer grade is known as a(n)   2._____

    A. elevator   B. ejector   C. sump   D. conveyer

3. A check valve in a piping system will   3._____

    A. permit excessive pressures in a boiler
    B. eliminate water hammer
    C. permit water to flow in only one direction
    D. control the rate of flow of water

4. The chemical MOST frequently used to clean drains clogged with grease is   4._____

    A. muriatic acid   B. soda ash
    C. ammonia   D. caustic soda

5. To test for leaks in a newly installed C.I. waste stack,   5._____

    A. oil of peppermint is poured into the top of the stack
    B. smoke under pressure is pumped into the stack
    C. a water meter is used to measure the water flow
    D. dye is placed in the system at the top of the stack

6. When installing a catch basin, the outlet should be located   6._____

    A. at the same level as the inlet
    B. above the inlet
    C. below the inlet
    D. at the invert

7. The copper float in a low down water tank is perforated so that water enters the ball. As a result, the tank will   7._____

    A. flush once, and then will not operate again
    B. not flush at all
    C. not flush completely
    D. continue to flush, but water will be wasted

8. If water leaks from the stem of a faucet when the faucet is opened, the _____ should be   8._____

    A. faucet; replaced   B. cap nut; rethreaded
    C. seat; reground   D. packing; replaced

9. In a hot water heating system, it may be necessary to *bleed* radiators to

   A. relieve high steam pressure
   B. permit entrapped, air to escape
   C. allow condensate to return to the boiler
   D. drain off waste water

10. When painting raw wood, puttying of nail holes should be done

    A. 24 hours before the prime coat
    B. immediately before the prime coat
    C. after the prime coat and before the second coat
    D. after the second coat and before the finish

11. In general, the one of the following that will dry *tack free* in the SHORTEST time is

    A. lacquer   B. varnish   C. enamel   D. oil paint

12. The *vehicle* MOST frequently used in paints for exterior wood surfaces is

    A. white lead   B. linseed oil
    C. japan   D. varnish

13. Painting of an interior plastered wall is usually delayed until the plaster is dry. If this practice is NOT followed, the paint might

    A. chalk   B. fade   C. run   D. blister

14. A *sealer* applied over knots and pitch streaks to prevent *bleeding* through paint is

    A. shellac   B. lacquer
    C. coal tar   D. carnauba wax

15. Painting of outside steel in near freezing (32° F) weather is poor practice MAINLY because

    A. the paint will not dry properly
    B. ice will form in the thinner
    C. more paint is required
    D. paint fumes are dangerous

16. When repainting exterior woodwork that has a glossy finish, good adhesion of paint is BEST obtained by first

    A. *washing* the work with diluted lye
    B. *dulling* the work with sandpaper
    C. *warming* the work with an electric heater
    D. *roughening* the work with a rasp

17. The one of the following methods of cleaning steelwork prior to painting that is NOT commonly used on exterior work, such as bridges, is

    A. sandblasting   B. flame cleaning
    C. wire brushing   D. pickling

18. When spraying oil paints, the type of gun and nozzle preferred is a _____ feed gun, _____ mix nozzle.

    A. pressure; internal
    B. pressure, external
    C. syphon; internal
    D. syphon; external

19. When opening a bag of cement, you find that the cement is lumpy.
    The cement should be

    A. discarded and not used at all
    B. crushed before placing in the mixer
    C. used as is since the mixer will grind it
    D. well mixed with water and stored overnight before using

20. A 1:2:4 concrete mix by volume is specified.
    If 6 cubic feet of cement is to be used in the mix, the volume of sand to use is, in cubic feet,

    A. 3   B. 6   C. 12   D. 24

21. Honeycombing in concrete is BEST prevented by

    A. increasing water-cement ratio
    B. heating concrete in cold weather
    C. using mechanical vibrators
    D. adding calcium chloride

22. When a lightweight concrete is required, the one of the following that is COMMONLY used as an aggregate is

    A. gravel   B. brick chips   C. stone   D. cinders

23. A rubbed finish on concrete is USUALLY obtained by use of a

    A. carborundum brick
    B. garnet sanding belt
    C. fibre brush and wax
    D. pad of steel wool

24. A copper strip is frequently embedded in the concrete across a construction joint in a concrete wall.
    The purpose of this is to

    A. make a watertight joint
    B. bond the two parts of the wall together
    C. prevent unequal settlement
    D. retard temperature cracking

25. In brickwork laid in common bond, a header course USUALLY occurs in every _____ course.

    A. 2nd   B. 4th   C. 6th   D. 8th

26. Pointing of brickwork refers to

    A. cutting brick to fit
    B. patching mortar joints
    C. attaching brick veneer
    D. arranging brick in an arch

27. Furring is applied to brick walls to

    A. strengthen the wall
    B. waterproof the wall
    C. provide ventilation to prevent condensation
    D. provide a base for lathing

28. The FIRST coat in plaster work is *scratched* in order to

    A. remove excess plaster
    B. smooth the base for the second coat
    C. provide a bond for the second coat
    D. strengthen the base coat

29. An alloy used where resistance to corrosion is important is

    A. tungsten   B. mild steel   C. monel   D. tin

30. The size of iron pipe is given in terms of its nominal

    A. weight   B. inside diameter
    C. outside diameter   D. wall thickness

31. When preparing surfaces to be soldered, the FIRST step is

    A. tinning   B. sweating   C. heating   D. cleaning

32. To test for leaks in an acetylene torch, it is BEST that one use

    A. soapy water   B. a match
    C. a gas with a strong odor D. a pressure gauge

33. One advantage of using a Pittsburgh lock seam when joining two pieces of sheet metal is that, once formed in the shop, it may be assembled anywhere with a

    A. hickey   B. swage   C. template   D. mallet

34. White cast iron is

    A. hard and brittle   B. hard and ductile
    C. ductile and malleable D. brittle and malleable

35. The gage used for measuring copper wire is

    A. U.S. Standard   B. Stubbs
    C. Washburn and Moen   D. Brown and Sharpe

36. The BEST flux to use when soldering copper wires in an electric circuit is

    A. sal ammoniac   B. zinc chloride
    C. rosin   D. borax

37. The spark test, to determine the approximate composition of an unknown metal, is made by

    A. holding the metal against a grinding wheel
    B. striking flint on the unknown metal
    C. connecting wires from a source of electric power to the metal and striking an arc with a bare wire
    D. heating with an oxyacetylene torch

38. The one of the following metals that is MOST commonly used for bearings is 38.____

    A. duraluminum   B. brass   C. babbit   D. lead

39. A *tailstock* is found on a 39.____

    A. drill press   B. shaper   C. planer   D. lathe

40. The BEST lubricant to use when cutting screw threads in steel is 40.____

    A. naphtha   B. 3-in-1 oil
    C. lard oil   D. linseed oil

41. When a high speed cutting tool is required, the tip is frequently made of 41.____

    A. carborundum   B. tungsten carbide
    C. bronze   D. vanadium

42. A nut is turned on a 3/4"-10 bolt.
    When the nut is turned five complete turns on this bolt, the distance it moves along the bolt 42.____

    A. depends on the type of thread   B. is 0.2 inches
    C. is 0.375 inches   D. is 0.5 inches

43. Of the following, the STRONGEST screw thread form is the 43.____

    A. Whitworth   B. Acme
    C. National Standard   D. V

44. *Knurling* refers to 44.____

    A. rolling depressions in a fixed pattern on a cylindrical surface
    B. turning between centers on a lathe
    C. making deep cuts in a flat plate with a milling machine
    D. drilling matching holes in bolt and nut for a cotter pin

45. A special device used to guide the drill as well as to hold the work when drilling is known as a 45.____

    A. dolly   B. jig   C. chuck   D. collet

46. Tools that have a *Morse taper* would be used on a 46.____

    A. milling machine   B. shaper
    C. planer   D. drill press

47. When tapping a blind hole in a plate, the FIRST tap to use is a 47.____

    A. plug   B. bottoming   C. lead   D. taper

48. An important safety practice to remember when cutting a rivet with a chisel is to wear 48.____

    A. leather gloves   B. steel toe shoes
    C. cup goggles   D. a hard hat

49. Electricians working around *live wires* should wear gloves made of

    A. asbestos   B. metal mesh   C. leather   D. rubber

50. Storage of oily rags presents a safety hazard because of possible

    A. fire
    B. poisonous flames
    C. attraction of rats
    D. leakage of oil

KEY (CORRECT ANSWERS)

1. A	11. A	21. C	31. D	41. B
2. B	12. B	22. D	32. A	42. D
3. C	13. D	23. A	33. D	43. B
4. D	14. A	24. A	34. A	44. A
5. B	15. A	25. C	35. B	45. B
6. C	16. B	26. B	36. C	46. D
7. D	17. D	27. D	37. A	47. D
8. D	18. A	28. C	38. C	48. C
9. B	19. A	29. C	39. D	49. D
10. C	20. C	30. B	40. C	50. A

TEST 2

DIRECTIONS: Each question or incomplete statement is followed by several suggested answers or completions. Select the one that BEST answers the question or completes the statement. *PRINT THE LETTER OF THE CORRECT ANSWER IN THE SPACE AT THE RIGHT.*

1. *Shimmying* of the front wheels of a truck is MOST frequently caused by   1.____

   A. worn front brake drums
   B. a worn differential gear
   C. a loose steering gear
   D. a dead shock absorber

2. The MOST important reason for maintaining correct air pressure in all tires of a truck is to   2.____

   A. prevent the truck from swerving when brakes are applied
   B. permit the truck to stop quicker in an emergency
   C. provide a smoother ride
   D. prevent excessive wear on the tires

3. The oil gage on the dashboard of a truck indicates   3.____

   A. the amount of oil in the pan
   B. the pressure at which the oil is being pumped
   C. if the oil filter is working
   D. the temperature of the oil in the motor

4. An unbalanced wheel on a truck is corrected by   4.____

   A. bending the rim slightly
   B. adjusting the king pin
   C. changing the ratio of caster to camber
   D. adding small weights to the rim

5. A cold motor on a truck should be warmed up in wintertime by   5.____

   A. turning on the heater and pouring warm water into the radiator
   B. allowing the motor to idle for a few minutes
   C. racing the motor
   D. alternately pressing the gas pedal to the floor and releasing it

6. The brake pedal on a truck goes to the floorboard when pushed. The one of the following that would cause this condition is   6.____

   A. air in the hydraulic system
   B. wet brakes
   C. excessive fluid in the cylinders
   D. a loose backing plate

7. The ammeter of a truck indicates no charge during operation even though the battery is run down. To find the fault, the generator field terminal is grounded. The ammeter now shows a charge. The part that is defective is the   7.____

   A. generator field coil
   B. armature
   C. brushes
   D. voltage regulator

45

8. The part used to control the ratio of air and gasoline in a truck engine is the

   A. bogie   B. filter   C. carburetor   D. pump

9. The MAIN purpose of a vacuum booster on a truck engine is to

   A. increase the manifold vacuum
   B. assist windshield wiper operation
   C. provide a steadier fuel flow
   D. govern engine speed

10. The purpose of grounding the frame of an electric motor is to

    A. prevent excessive vibration
    B. eliminate shock hazards
    C. reduce power requirements
    D. prevent overheating

11. The one of the following that is NOT part of an electric motor is a

    A. brush   B. rheostat   C. pole   D. commutator

12. An electrical transformer would be used to

    A. change current from AC to DC
    B. raise or lower the power
    C. raise or lower the voltage
    D. change the frequency

13. The piece of equipment that would be rated in ampere hours is a

    A. storage battery
    B. bus bar
    C. rectifier
    D. capacitor

14. A ballast is a necessity in a(n)

    A. motor generator set
    B. fluorescent lighting system
    C. oil circuit breaker
    D. synchronous converter

15. The power factor in an AC circuit is on when

    A. no current is flowing
    B. the voltage at the source is a minimum
    C. the voltage and current are in phase
    D. there is no load

16. Neglecting the internal resistance in the battery, the current flowing through the battery shown in the sketch above is _____ amp. (Circuit: 6V battery with 1 OHM and 1 OHM resistors)

    A. 3   B. 6   C. 9   D. 12

17. When excess current flows, a circuit breaker is opened directly by the action of a

    A. condenser   B. transistor   C. relay   D. solenoid

18. The MAIN purpose of bridging in building floor construction is to

    A. spread floor loads evenly to joists
    B. reduce the number of joists required
    C. permit use of thinner subflooring
    D. reduce noise passage through floors

19. Of the following, the material MOST commonly used for subflooring is

    A. rock lath   B. insulation board
    C. plywood   D. transite

20. In connection with stair construction, the one of the following that is LEAST related to the others is

    A. tread   B. cap   C. nosing   D. riser

21. The type of nail MOST commonly used in flooring is

    A. common   B. cut   C. brad   D. casing

22. The edge joint of flooring boards is COMMONLY

    A. mortise and tenon   B. shiplap
    C. half lap   D. tongue and groove

23. The purpose of a ridge board in building construction is to

    A. locate corners of a building
    B. keep plaster work smooth
    C. support the ends of roof rafters
    D. conceal openings at the eaves

24. To prevent splintering of wood when using an auger bit,

    A. the bit should be hollow ground
    B. hold the piece of wood in a vise
    C. clamp a piece of scrap wood to the back of the piece being drilled
    D. use a slow speed on the drill press

25. End grain of a post can be MOST easily planed by use of a _____ plane.

    A. rafter   B. jack   C. fore   D. block

26. A butt gauge is used when

    A. hanging doors   B. laying out stairs
    C. making rafter cuts   D. framing studs

27. The one of the following grades of sandpaper with the FINEST grit is

    A. 0   B. 2/0   C. 1/2   D. 1

28. The sum of the following numbers, 3 7/8, 14 1/4, 6 7/16, 22 3/16, 8 1/2 is

    A. 55 1/16   B. 55 1/8   C. 55 3/16   D. 55 1/4

29. The area of the rectangular field shown in the diagram at the right is, in square feet,
    A. 29,456
    B. 29,626
    C. 29,716
    D. 29,836

    437 FT.

    68 ft

30. The cost of material is approximately 3/8ths of the total cost of a certain job. If the total cost of the job is $127.56, then the cost of material is MOST NEARLY

    A. $47.83   B. $48.24   C. $48.65   D. $49.06

31. A blueprint is drawn to a scale of 1/4" = 1'0". A line on the blueprint that is not dimensioned is measured with a ruler and found to be 3 3/8" long.
    The length represented by this line is

    A. 13'2"   B. 13'4"   C. 13'6"   D. 13'8"

32. A maintainer, in repairing a brick wall, spends one-half hour getting materials, forty-three minutes chipping and cleaning the wall, fifteen minutes mixing the mortar, and one hour and twenty-seven minutes in applying the brick and finishing.
    The total time spent on this repair job is _____ hours _____ minute(s).

    A. 2; 45   B. 2; 50   C. 2; 55   D. 3; 0

33. *Employees are responsible for the good care, proper maintenance, and serviceable condition of property issued or assigned to their use.*
    As used above, *serviceable condition* means MOST NEARLY

    A. capable of being repaired
    B. fit for use
    C. ease of handling
    D. minimum cost

34. *An employee shall be on the alert constantly for potential accident hazards.*
    As used above, *potential* means MOST NEARLY

    A. dangerous   B. careless   C. possible   D. frequent

Questions 35-37.

DIRECTIONS: Questions 35 to 37, inclusive, are to be answered in accordance with the following paragraph.

All cement work contracts, more or less, in setting. The contraction in concrete walls and other structures causes fine cracks to develop at regular intervals. The tendency to contract increases in direct proportion to the quantity of cement in the concrete. A rich mixture will contract more than a lean mixture. A concrete wall, which has been made of a very lean mixture and which has been built by filling only about one foot in depth of concrete in the form each day will frequently require close inspection to reveal the cracks.

35. According to the above paragraph,

    A. shrinkage seldom occurs in concrete
    B. shrinkage occurs only in certain types of concrete
    C. by placing concrete at regular intervals, shrinkage may be avoided
    D. it is impossible to prevent shrinkage

36. According to the above paragraph, the one of the factors which reduces shrinkage in concrete is the

    A. volume of concrete in wall
    B. height of each day's pour
    C. length of wall
    D. length and height of wall

37. According to the above paragraph, a rich mixture

    A. pours the easiest
    B. shows the largest amount of cracks
    C. is low in cement content
    D. need not be inspected since cracks are few

Questions 38-39.

DIRECTIONS: Questions 38 and 39 are to be answered in accordance with the following paragraph.

Painting is done to preserve surfaces, and unless the surface is properly prepared, good preservation will not be possible. Apply paint only to clean dry surfaces. After a surface has been scaled, which means that all loose paint and rust are removed by chipping, scraping, and wire brushing, be sure all dust and dirt are completely removed.

38. According to the above paragraph, the MAIN purpose of painting a wall is to _____ the wall.

    A. clean   B. waterproof
    C. protect   D. remove dust from

39. According to the above paragraph,

    A. chipping, scraping, and wire brushing are the only methods permitted for cleaning surfaces
    B. painting is effective only when the surface is clean
    C. scaling refers only to the removal of rust
    D. paint may be applied on wet surfaces

40. The order in which the dimensions of stock are listed on a bill of materials is

    A. thickness, length, and width   B. thickness, width, and length
    C. width, length, and thickness   D. length, thickness, and width

41. The glue that will BEST withstand extreme exposure to moisture and water is _____ glue.

    A. polyvinyl
    B. resorcinol
    C. powdered resin
    D. protein

42. Four board feet of lumber, listed at $350.00 per M, will cost

    A. $3.50   B. $1.40   C. $1.30   D. $4.00

43. The cap iron or chip breaker stiffens the plane iron and

    A. protects the cutting edge
    B. curls the shaving
    C. regulates the thickness of the shaving
    D. reduces mouth gap

44. Coping-saw blades have teeth shaped like those on a _____ saw.

    A. dovetail   B. crosscut   C. back   D. rip

45. Of the following, the claw hammer that is BEST suited for general use in a woodworking shop is the _____ claw.

    A. straight
    B. bell-faced curved
    C. plain-faced curved
    D. adze eye curved

46. The natural binder which cements wood fibers together and makes wood solid is

    A. cellulose
    B. lignin
    C. alpha-cellulose
    D. trichocarpa

47. The plane that is BEST suited for trimming the bottom of a dado or lap joint is the _____ plane.

    A. block   B. router   C. rabbet   D. core-box

48. Brads are fasteners that are similar to _____ nails.

    A. escutcheon
    B. box
    C. finishing
    D. duplex head

49. The plane in which the plane iron is inserted with its bevel in the up position is the _____ plane.

    A. fore   B. rabbet   C. block   D. circular

50. Coating materials used to protect wood against fire USUALLY contain a water soluble fire-retardant such as

    A. ammonium chloride
    B. sodium perborate
    C. sodium silicate
    D. sal soda

KEY (CORRECT ANSWERS)

1. C	11. B	21. B	31. C	41. B
2. D	12. C	22. D	32. C	42. B
3. B	13. A	23. C	33. B	43. B
4. D	14. B	24. C	34. C	44. D
5. B	15. C	25. D	35. D	45. B
6. A	16. A	26. A	36. B	46. B
7. D	17. D	27. B	37. B	47. B
8. C	18. A	28. D	38. C	48. C
9. B	19. C	29. C	39. B	49. C
10. B	20. B	30. A	40. B	50. C

EXAMINATION SECTION
TEST 1

DIRECTIONS: Each question or incomplete statement is followed by several suggested answers or completions. Select the one that BEST answers the question or completes the statement. *PRINT THE LETTER OF THE CORRECT ANSWER IN THE SPACE AT THE RIGHT.*

1. A shrink fitted collar is to be removed from a shaft. One good way to do this would be to drive out the shaft after _____ collar.

    A. *chilling* only the
    B. *chilling* both the shaft and
    C. *heating* only the
    D. *heating* both the shaft and

2. It is CORRECT to say that

    A. a standard brick weighs about 8 lbs.
    B. the dimensions of a common brick are 8" x 3 3/4" x 2 1/4"
    C. vertical joints in a brick wall are called bed joints
    D. in laying bricks the head joints should be slushed with mortar

3. A snail pump impeller is checked for static balance by

    A. running the pump at high speed and listening for rubs
    B. mounting it on parallel and level knife edges and noting if it turns
    C. weighing it and comparing the weight against the original weight
    D. putting it on a lathe to see if it runs true

4. The sum of the following dimensions: 3' x 2 1/4", 8 7/8", 2'6 3/8", 2'9 3/4", and 1'0" is

    A. 16'7 1/4"   B. 10'7 1/4"   C. 10'3 1/4"   D. 9'3 1/4"

5. A requisition for nails was worded as follows: *100 lbs., 10d, 3 inch, common wive nails, galvanized.*
   The UNNECESSARY information in this requisition is

    A. 100 lbs.   B. common   C. galvanized   D. 3 inch

6. Electric arc welding is COMMONLY done by the use of _____ voltage and _____ amperage.

    A. *low; high*   B. *high; high*
    C. *high; low*   D. *low; low*

7. A GOOD principle for you to follow after teaching a maintenance procedure to a new helper is to

    A. tell him that you expect him to make many mistakes at first
    B. observe his work procedure and point out any errors he may make
    C. have him write out the procedure from memory
    D. assume he knows the procedure if he asks no questions

8. Multiple threads are used on the stems of some large valves to

   A. reduce the effort required to open the valve
   B. prevent binding of the valve stem
   C. secure faster opening and closing of the valve
   D. decrease the length of stem travel

9. After the base plate of a new machine has been fitted over the foundation bolts, it should be leveled by

   A. inserting steel shims under the plate
   B. chipping the high spots off the floor
   C. using thin cement grout under the plate
   D. grinding down the high spots on the base plate

10. In nixing concrete by hand, the materials are first thoroughly mixed dry and then mixed with water. This is a good procedure because it

    A. caves cement
    B. reduces the amount of water required
    C. avoids settling of the aggregate
    D. properly coats the aggregate with the cement

11. A revolution counter applied to the end of a rotating shaft reads 100 when a stopwatch is started and 850 after 90 seconds.
    The shaft is rotating at a speed of _____ rpm.

    A. 500   B. 633   C. 750   D. 950

12. If a kink develops in a wire rope, it would be BEST to

    A. hammer out the kink with a lead hammer
    B. straighten out the kink by putting it in a vise and applying sufficient pressure
    C. discard the portion of the rope containing the kink
    D. keep the rope in use and allow the kink to work itself out

13. Steel pipe posts have been placed into prepared holes in concrete.
    To properly secure the posts, they should be caulked inplace with

    A. molten lead   B. cement mortar
    C. oakum   D. hot pitch

14. The PRINCIPAL reason for grounding of electrical equipment is to

    A. save power   B. guard against shock
    C. prevent open circuits D. prevent short circuits

15. A spirit level has been dropped and a deep indentation made in the wood.
    The BEST thing to do is to

    A. ignore the incident if the bubbles were not broken
    B. sand down the surface to remove the indentation
    C. get a new level
    D. test the level

16. A strike plate is MOST closely associated with a 16.____

    A. lock B. sash weight
    C. hinge D. door check

17. You receive a special assignment from your superior calling for the use of a type of wood 17.____
    which in your opinion is not suitable for the job.
    You should

    A. substitute the wood you believe to be most suitable
    B. carry out the order as received
    C. immediately call this to his attention
    D. consult another maintainer on what to do

18. A motor driven centrifugal pump takes water from a city main and delivers it to the noz- 18.____
    zles of a train washing machine. With little change in motor speed or suction pressure,
    the discharge pressure rises and the flow of cleaning water falls to a trickle.
    The PROBABLE cause is a

    A. failure of the impeller shaft
    B. leak in the piping between the pressure gage point of attachment and the nozzles
    C. blockage of the impeller
    D. blockage between the pressure gage point of attachment and the nozzles

19. A standard hoisting rope size is designated as 6 x 19. This indicates that the rope has 19.____

    A. 6 strands, each made of 19 wires
    B. 19 strands, each made of 6 wires
    C. 6 strands of No. 19 gage wire
    D. 19 strands of No. 6 gage wire

20. The two planes which make up the MOST useful combination 20.____
    for general carpentry work are the _____ plane and the _____ plane.

    A. jack; jointer B. jack; block
    C. smooth; block D. fore; jointer

21. If you were drilling a structural plate and the drill cuttings were in the form of long contin- 21.____
    uous shavings, you could rightly conclude that the

    A. drill point was too sharp
    B. material being drilled was wrought iron
    C. bearing pressure on the drill was insufficient
    D. drilling was being done correctly

22. Studs and joists for light building construction are USUALLY spaced on _____ inch cen- 22.____
    ters.

    A. 12 B. 14 C. 16 D. 18

23. If power driven rivets are loose, the MOST likely reason would be that the rivets were 23.____

    A. too long
    B. too short
    C. driven with high air pressure
    D. overheated

24. If a drawing for a pipe installation is made to a scale of 1 1/2" to the foot, the drawing is said to be one _____ size.

    A. half   B. quarter   C. eighth   D. sixteenth

25. A gear train consists of a driver with 120 teeth, an idler with 60 teeth, and a driven gear with 200 teeth. If the driver rotates at 1500 rpm, the driven gear rotates at _____ rpm.

    A. 225   B. 900   C. 2500   D. 10,000

26. A certain pipe fitting is marked *200 WOG*. This fitting could NOT properly be used in a pipe line for _____ pounds gage maximum.

    A. steam at 200   B. water at 150
    C. air at 200   D. oil at 150

27. A file having two *safe* edges is COMMONLY known as a _____ file.

    A. flat   B. mill   C. hand   D. pillar

28. By trial, it is found that by using 2 cubic feet of sand, a 5 cubic foot batch of concrete is produced.
    Using the same proportions, the amount of sand, in cubic feet, required to produce 2 cubic yards of concrete is MOST NEARLY

    A. 7   B. 22   C. 27   D. 45

29. Tooling of the face joints of a brick wall under construction should be done

    A. after the mortar has acquired its initial set
    B. after the entire wall is laid
    C. after the mortar has acquired its final set
    D. as each brick is laid

30. A gland bushing is associated in practice with a(n)

    A. gas engine   B. electric motor
    C. centrifugal pump   D. lathe

31. A house drain is successively offset by means of a 1/8 bend, a 1/16 bend, and a 1/32 bend.
    The total angular offset of this line is MOST NEARLY

    A. 34°   B. 39°   C. 68°   D. 79°

32. The flushing mechanism in a low tank water closet is so arranged that a fill tube supplies water from the ball cock to the overflow standpipe for a short interval immediately after the closet is flushed.
    The MAIN reason for this is to

    A. finish cleaning the water passages of the closet
    B. properly seal the ball in its seat
    C. renew the seal in the closet trap
    D. scour the flush tube from the tank to the closet

33. A job calls for the setting of wrought iron pipe sleeves in concrete floor construction for the passage of water risers.
In order to provide for the passage of a 2" riser, the MINIMUM diameter of the sleeve is

    A. 2 1/2"   B. 3"   C. 4"   D. 5"

34. When applied to lumber, the designation *S4S* means

    A. all sides are rough
    B. all four sides are of the same size
    C. fourth grade lumber
    D. all sides are dressed

35. To guard against accidents in connection with wood scaffolding,

    A. inspect the nailing before the scaffold is loaded
    B. never put a heavy load on a scaffold
    C. use only heavy timber for scaffold construction
    D. do not build high scaffolds

36. A reducing tee has one run opening of 2 inches, the second run opening of 1 1/2 inches, and the branch opening of 1 inch.
This tee would be specified as

    A. 1 x 1 1/2 x 2   B. 1 x 2 x 1 1/2
    C. 2 x 1 1/2 x 1   D. 2 x 1 x 1 1/2

37. A length of pipe is to be fitted with a 90° elbow at each end. The center to center distance between elbows is to be 4'6". The center to end dimension of each elbow is 2" and the thread engagement is 1/2".
The length to which the pipe should be cut is

    A. 4'1"   B. 4'2"   C. 4'3"   D. 4'4 1/2"

38. Sheet metal seams are sometimes grooved. The MAIN function of the grooving is to

    A. facilitate making a soldered joint
    B. prevent unlocking
    C. improve the appearance of the joint
    D. save sheet metal

39. When fitting new piston rings in a compressor, the piston ring gap is BEST measured by means of a(n)

    A. feeler gage   B. inside caliper
    C. 6" rule   D. depth gage

40. The ampere-hour rating of a battery depends MAINLY on the

    A. number of cells connected in series
    B. casing composition
    C. quantity of electrolyte
    D. number and area of the battery plates

KEY (CORRECT ANSWERS)

1. C	11. A	21. D	31. D
2. B	12. C	22. C	32. C
3. B	13. A	23. B	33. B
4. C	14. B	24. C	34. D
5. D	15. D	25. B	35. A
6. A	16. A	26. A	36. C
7. B	17. C	27. D	37. C
8. C	18. D	28. B	38. B
9. A	19. A	29. A	39. A
10. D	20. B	30. C	40. D

TEST 2

DIRECTIONS: Each question or incomplete statement is followed by several suggested answers or completions. Select the one that BEST answers the question or completes the statement. *PRINT THE LETTER OF THE CORRECT ANSWER IN THE SPACE AT THE RIGHT.*

1. In making a high wooden scaffold, proper splices in 2 x 4 lumber which is to be used vertically would be made by   1.____

    A. lapping each joint with a cleat below
    B. butting the ends and boxing in the joints with 1" boards
    C. butting the ends and nailing a 2 x 4 over the splice
    D. making half-lap joints

2. With respect to soldering, it is LEAST important that   2.____

    A. the soldering copper be clean and well-tinned
    B. a good flux suitable for the metal being soldered be used
    C. the joint to be soldered be well-cleaned
    D. a lot of solder be used

3. When two sheet metal plates are riveted together, a specified minimum distance must be provided from the edge of each plate to the nearest line of rivets in order to prevent   3.____

    A. the rivet heads from working loose
    B. the rivets from being sheared
    C. tearing of the material between the rivets and the edges of the plates
    D. excessive stress on the rivets

4. A hoisting cable is wound on a 14" drum which is rotating at 5 rpm.   4.____
   The load being raised by this cable will move at an APPROXIMATE linear speed, in feet per minute, of

    A. 13.5   B. 18.3   C. 70   D. 220

5. Spreaders are used in connection with forms for concrete to   5.____

    A. hold the walls of a form the correct distance apart
    B. anchor a form to the ground
    C. make a form watertight
    D. make the cement spread evenly through the form

6. By curing of concrete is meant   6.____

    A. finishing the surface of the concrete
    B. softening stiff concrete by adding water
    C. keeping the concrete wet while setting
    D. the salvaging of frozen concrete

7. If steel weighs 480 lbs. per cubic foot, the weight of an 18" x 18" x 2" steel base plate is _____ lbs.   7.____

    A. 180   B. 216   C. 427   D. 648

8. Standard wrought iron pipe and extra strong wrought iron pipe of the same nominal size differ in

   A. outside diameter
   B. inside diameter
   C. chemical composition
   D. threading

9. Plumbing system stacks are vented to the atmosphere. These stacks will NOT

   A. relieve the back pressure on traps from the sewer side
   B. prevent the siphoning of traps
   C. ventilate the drainage system
   D. prevent the sewer from backing up into the fixtures

10. The MOST likely cause of accidents involving minor injuries is

    A. careless work practices
    B. lack of safety devices
    C. inferior equipment and material
    D. insufficient safety posters

11. In the maintenance of shop equipment, lubrication should be done

    A. periodically
    B. only if necessary
    C. whenever time permits
    D. only during the overhaul period

12. The total number of cubic yards of earth to be removed to nake a trench 3'9" wide, 25'0" long, and 4'3" deep is MOST NEARLY

    A. 53.1   B. 35.4   C. 26.6   D. 11.8

13. A large number of 2 x 4 studs, some 10'5" long and some 6'5 1/2" long, are required for a job.
    To minimize waste, it would be preferable to order lengths of _____ ft.

    A. 16   B. 17   C. 18   D. 19

14. A 6" pipe is connected to a 4" pipe through a reducer. If 100 cubic feet of water is flowing through the 6" pipe per minute, the flow, in cubic feet per minute, through the 4" pipe is

    A. 225   B. 100   C. 66.6   D. 44.4

15. The type of seam generally used in the construction of sheet metal cylinders of small diameters is the _____ seam.

    A. double edged
    B. folded
    C. double hemmed
    D. simple lap

16. Two branch ventilating ducts, one 12 inches square and the other 18 inches square, are to connect to a square main duct.
    In order to maintain the same cross-sectional area, the dimension of the main duct should be _____ inches square.

    A. 14   B. 20   C. 24   D. 28

17. In reference to preparing mortar, it is CORRECT to say that the lime used

    A. may burn the skin
    B. hastens setting
    C. prevents absorption of water by the brick
    D. decreases the amount of water needed

18. The intercooler of a two-stage air compressor is connected to the compressor unit

    A. before the air intake pipe to the first stage
    B. between the second stage and the receiver
    C. between the two stages
    D. after the receiver.

19. In oxyacetylene welding, the hose that is connected to the oxygen cylinder is USUALLY colored

    A. yellow   B. white   C. purple   D. green

20. When bonding new concrete to old concrete, the surface of the old concrete should be

    A. left untouched   B. dry
    C. carefully smoothed   D. chipped and roughened

21. A sack of Portland cement is considered to have a volume, in cubic feet, of

    A. 1/2   B. 3/4   C. 1   D. 14

22. The purpose of a vacuum breaker used with an automatic flush valve is to

    A. limit the flow of water to the fixture
    B. prevent pollution of the water supply
    C. equalize the water pressure
    D. control the water pressure to the fixture

23. Wiping solder for lead pipe USUALLY has a melting range of _____ °F.

    A. 150 to 250   B. 251 to 350
    C. 360 to 470   D. 475 to 600

24. A space heater is to be suspended from a structural beam. The heater should be suspended by a hanger

    A. passing through a hole in the web of the beam
    B. passing through a hole in the flange of the beam
    C. welded to the beam
    D. clamped to the beam

25. With respect to babbitted sleeve bearings, oil grooves are

    A. cut only on the top half
    B. cut only on the bottom half
    C. cut on both halves
    D. never necessary

26. When an employee finds it necessary to work near a live third rail, it is BEST to cover the third rail with a

    A. rubber mat
    B. canvas cloth
    C. board
    D. sheet of heavy paper

27. A 10-inch foundation wall is 11 feet long and 15 feet high. If the compressive strength of the wall is 300 pounds per square inch, the MAXIMUM permissible load on this wall is _____ lbs.

    A. 540,000
    B. 495,000
    C. 396,000
    D. 33,000

28. It is INCORRECT to state that

    A. neat cement contains cement and water
    B. salt is used to hasten the setting of concrete
    C. the strength of concrete is affected by the water ratio
    D. a sidewalk should slope toward the street

29. When sharpening a hand saw, the FIRST operation is to file the teeth so that they are of the same height. This is known as

    A. shaping
    B. setting
    C. leveling
    D. jointing

30. The swing of a lathe is the

    A. diameter of the largest piece that can be turned
    B. distance between centers of the head and tail spindles
    C. size of the face plate
    D. radius of the chuck

31. Assume that the lead screw, stud gear, and spindle of a lathe revolve at the same speed. It is required to cut 10 threads per inch when the lead screw has 6 threads per inch. If the stud gear has 48 teeth, the lead screw gear must have _____ teeth.

    A. 48
    B. 60
    C. 64
    D. 80

32. The safety device used on a crane to prevent overtravel is called a(n)

    A. unloader
    B. governor
    C. limit switch
    D. overload relay

33. It is INCORRECT to say that

    A. there is a difference between fittings for threaded drainage pipe and fittings for ordinary threaded pipe
    B. a gasoline torch must be fully filled with gasoline
    C. *Red Brass* pipe contains about 85% copper
    D. loose parts in a faucet may cause noisy operation

34. A requisition for lag screws does NOT require stating the

    A. diameter
    B. quantity
    C. threads per inch
    D. length

35. In an accident report, the information which may be MOST useful in decreasing the recurrence of similar type accidents is the

    A. extent of injuries sustained
    B. time the accident happened
    C. number of people involved
    D. cause of the accident

36. Carbon tetrachloride is NOT recommended for cleaning purposes because of

    A. the poisonous nature of its fumes
    B. its limited cleaning value
    C. the damaging effects it has on equipment
    D. the difficulty of application

37. The part of the thread directly measured with a thread micrometer is the

    A. thread height
    B. major diameter
    C. thread lead
    D. pitch diameter

38. The side support for steps or stairs is called a

    A. ledger board
    B. runner
    C. stringer
    D. riser

39. A sheet metal plate has been cut in the form of a right triangle with sides of 5, 12, and 13 inches.
    The area of this plate, in square inches, is

    A. 30
    B. 32 1/2
    C. 60
    D. 78

40. The BEST first aid for a man who has no external injury but is apparently suffering from internal injury due to an accident is to

    A. take him at once to a doctor's office
    B. make him comfortable and immediately summon a doctor or ambulance
    C. administer a stimulant
    D. start artificial respiration

KEY (CORRECT ANSWERS)

1.	B	11.	A	21.	C	31.	D
2.	D	12.	D	22.	B	32.	C
3.	C	13.	C	23.	C	33.	B
4.	B	14.	B	24.	D	34.	C
5.	A	15.	D	25.	A	35.	D
6.	C	16.	B	26.	A	36.	A
7.	A	17.	A	27.	C	37.	D
8.	B	18.	C	28.	B	38.	C
9.	D	19.	D	29.	D	39.	A
10.	A	20.	D	30.	A	40.	B

EXAMINATION SECTION
TEST 1

DIRECTIONS: Each question or incomplete statement is followed by several suggested answers or completions. Select the one that BEST answers the question or completes the statement. *PRINT THE LETTER OF THE CORRECT ANSWER IN THE SPACE AT THE RIGHT.*

1. Of the following, the one that is a grease fitting is a _____ fitting. 1.____

   A. Morse
   B. Brown and Sharpe
   C. Zerk
   D. Caliper

2. In an automobile equipped with an ammeter, the ammeter is used to 2.____

   A. indicate current flow
   B. regulate current flow
   C. act as a circuit breaker
   D. measure engine r.p.m.

3. The ignition points in the distributor of a gasoline engine are opened by means of a 3.____

   A. spring
   B. vacuum
   C. cam with lobes
   D. gear

4. MOST automobile engines that use gasoline as fuel operate as _____ cycle engines. 4.____

   A. single
   B. single stroke, single
   C. two-stroke, two-
   D. four-stroke, two-

5. When making a hole in a concrete floor for a machine hold-down bolt, the BEST tool to use is a 5.____

   A. star drill
   B. drift punch
   C. cold chisel
   D. counterboring tool

6. When cutting a hole through a 1/2-inch thick wooden partition, the BEST type of saw to use from among the following choices is a _____ saw. 6.____

   A. coping   B. back   C. rip   D. saber

7. An anodized finish is USUALLY associated with 7.____

   A. aluminum
   B. steel
   C. cast iron
   D. brass

8. Certain devices are used to transmit power from one shaft to another. A device that does so WITHOUT the use of friction is a 8.____

   A. square jaw clutch
   B. simple disk clutch
   C. compression coupling
   D. thermocouple

9. If it is necessary to check the true temperature setting of a thermostat for a shop unit heater, it would be BEST to use 9.____

   A. a mercury thermometer near the heater
   B. a mercury thermometer near the thermostat

C. another similar thermostat near the thermostat to be tested
D. a standard thermostat

10. To remove a shrink-fitted collar from a shaft, it would be EASIEST to drive out the shaft after

   A. *chilling* the collar and heating the shaft
   B. *chilling* only the collar
   C. *heating* only the collar
   D. *heating* both the collar and the shaft

11. When drilling a hole in a broken machine stud in order to remove the stud with an extractor, it is BEST to drill the hole

   A. off-center
   B. in the center
   C. with the smallest diameter drill possible
   D. with a taper

12. When fitting two steel parts together, steel dowel pins are GENERALLY used to

   A. keep the parts securely fastened together
   B. provide a wide tolerance fit
   C. provide an adjustable clearance space between the two parts
   D. secure exact placement of these parts with respect to each other

13. When storing files, it is important that they do not touch each other. The PRIMARY reason for this is to prevent

   A. damage to the handles
   B. dirt from collecting in the teeth
   C. damage to the teeth
   D. rusting

14. The frequency of lubrication of bearings and other moving parts of machinery depends PRIMARILY on

   A. the amount of their use
   B. their size
   C. the direction of motion
   D. the operator's judgment

15. To determine whether the surface of a work bench is horizontal, the BEST tool to use is a

   A. surface gage
   B. plumb bob
   C. feeler gage
   D. spirit level

16. The swing on a lathe refers to the

   A. distance between centers of the head and tail spindles
   B. size of the face plate
   C. speed range of the gears in r.p.m.
   D. diameter of the largest workpiece that can be turned

17. When installing new piston rings in an air compressor, the piston ring gap is BEST measured by using a(n)

    A. outside caliper
    B. feeler gage
    C. depth gage
    D. inside caliper

18. When cutting external threads on a pipe, the tool that ACTUALLY cuts the thread is called a

    A. tap   B. die   C. reamer   D. hone

19. A dynamometer would be MOST useful in

    A. measuring angles on a steel plate
    B. determining the operating efficiency of an engine
    C. pumping hot fluids out of a tank
    D. heating large shop areas

20. A screw-thread micrometer is used PRIMARILY to measure

    A. pitch diameter
    B. thread height
    C. major diameter
    D. thread lead

21. A compound-pressure gage found on certain types of equipment is used to indicate

    A. the sum of two pressures
    B. the difference between two pressures
    C. either vacuum or pressure
    D. two different pressures simultaneously

22. Of the following, the machine screw having the SMALLEST diameter is

    A. 6-32 x 1 1/2"
    B. 8-32 x 3/4"
    C. 10-24 x 1"
    D. 12-24 x 1/2"

23. A good quality precision compression spring would MOST probably have

    A. a small diameter and small wire size
    B. its ends ground flat
    C. a large diameter and large wire size
    D. a high spring rate

24. From among the following materials, the MOST fireproof one for use in maintenance work is

    A. canvas   B. nylon   C. cotton   D. asbestos

25. The metal which has the GREATEST tendency to crack when dropped onto a hard surface is

    A. rolled steel
    B. forged steel
    C. wrought iron
    D. cast iron

26. When using a portable electric drill having a 3-conductor cord, it is IMPORTANT from a safety point of view that

    A. the drill is run at fairly slow speeds
    B. high-speed drill bits should be used

C. the power outlet has a ground connection
D. the drill is run on 3-phase current

27. The MOST efficient way of laying out a 25-foot long, straight line on a concrete floor is to

   A. use a carpenter's pencil and a steel tape
   B. lay out a cord and mark the line with a crayon
   C. use chalk and a 6-foot ruler
   D. snap it on with a chalked mason's line

28. The MAIN advantage of using pipes instead of timber for temporary scaffolding is that pipe scaffolding

   A. requires no painting
   B. is easier to assemble and disassemble
   C. requires no bracing
   D. looks better

29. In order to avoid damage to an air compressor, the air coming into it is USUALLY

   A. cooled   B. metered   C. filtered   D. heated

30. If a gear having 24 teeth is revolving at 150 r.p.m., then the speed of an 8-tooth pinion driving the gear is _____ r.p.m.

   A. 50   B. 300   C. 450   D. 1200

31. To preserve wood from rotting, it is BEST to use

   A. aluminum paint   B. red lead
   C. rosin   D. creosote

32. On a two-stage air compressor, the intercooler is connected to the compressor unit

   A. *between* the two stages
   B. *after* the second stage
   C. *before* the first stage
   D. *between* the receiver and the outlet

33. Teflon is COMMONLY used as a(n)

   A. protective coating on ceramic plumbing fixtures
   B. sealer on threaded pipe joints
   C. additive to engine lubricating oil
   D. penetrating oil for rusting parts

34. A marline spike is GENERALLY used to

   A. splice manila rope
   B. fasten a heavy metal part to a wood panel wall
   C. shift large crates
   D. anchor wooden items to a concrete wall

35. A screw having double threads is one that 35.____

    A. should never be used for fastening sheet metal parts
    B. has two parallel threads running in the same direction
    C. has a right hand and a left hand thread
    D. can be used with a mating single-threaded nut

36. If the diameter of a circular piece of sheet metal is 1 1/2 feet, the area, in square inches, 36.____
    is MOST NEARLY

    A. 1.77   B. 2.36   C. 254   D. 324

37. When removing a cartridge-type fuse from the fuse clips in a circuit, it is important to use 37.____
    a fuse-puller PRIMARILY to avoid

    A. blowing the fuse   B. damaging the fuse
    C. arcing   D. personal injury

38. The MOST probable cause for the breaking of a drill bit while drilling into a steel plate is 38.____

    A. excessive drill pressure
    B. a hard spot in the steel
    C. a drill speed which is too low
    D. too much cutting-oil lubricant

39. In assembling structural steel, a drift pin is used to 39.____

    A. line up holes
    B. punch holes
    C. temporarily hold welded parts
    D. knock out structural bolts

40. The TIGHTEST fit for a mating shaft and hole is a _____ fit. 40.____

    A. running   B. sliding   C. working   D. force

KEY (CORRECT ANSWERS)

1.	C	11.	B	21.	C	31.	D
2.	A	12.	D	22.	A	32.	A
3.	C	13.	C	23.	B	33.	B
4.	D	14.	A	24.	D	34.	A
5.	A	15.	D	25.	D	35.	B
6.	D	16.	D	26.	C	36.	C
7.	A	17.	B	27.	D	37.	D
8.	A	18.	B	28.	B	38.	A
9.	B	19.	B	29.	C	39.	A
10.	C	20.	A	30.	C	40.	D

TEST 2

DIRECTIONS: Each question or incomplete statement is followed by several suggested answers or completions. Select the one that BEST answers the question or completes the statement. *PRINT THE LETTER OF THE CORRECT ANSWER IN THE SPACE AT THE RIGHT.*

1. The crankshaft in a gasoline engine is PRIMARILY used to 1.____

    A. change reciprocating motion to rotary motion
    B. operate the valve lifters
    C. supply power to each cylinder
    D. function as a flywheel

2. Copper tubing is GENERALLY used in an annealed condition because annealing 2.____

    A. gives the copper tubing a protective finish
    B. makes the copper tubing harder
    C. provides a smoother surface on the inner and outer walls
    D. makes the copper tubing more ductile

3. Of the following, the MOST important advantage of a ratchet wrench as compared to an open-end wrench is that the ratchet wrench 3.____

    A. is adjustable
    B. cannot strip the threads of a nut
    C. can be used in a limited space
    D. measures the force applied

4. To provide a close-fitting hole for a taper pin, it is BEST to first drill the hole and then to use the appropriate 4.____

    A. hone   B. reamer
    C. boring tool D. counterboring tool

5. If a part that is being checked for size fits loosely into a *NO-GO* gauge, it means that the 5.____

    A. part is the proper size
    B. part must be made smaller
    C. part is the wrong size
    D. gauge should be tightened

6. A hacksaw blade with 32 teeth per inch is BEST for cutting 6.____

    A. materials less than 1/8-inch thick
    B. a 3-inch diameter brass bar
    C. 1" thick copper plates
    D. a 3-inch diameter steel bar

7. The BEST method to follow in order to prevent a drill from wandering upon starting to drill a hole in a steel plate is to 7.____

    A. use a high-speed drill
    B. first use a center-punch

C. use a drill with even cutting angles
D. exert heavy pressure when drilling

8. When grinding a tool, it is GOOD practice to keep moving the tool across the face of the grinding wheel in order to

   A. prevent the tool from becoming too hot
   B. avoid sparks
   C. maintain a uniform grinding speed
   D. prevent grooving the wheel

9. A material that is COMMONLY used as a lining for bearings in order to reduce friction is

   A. magnesium   B. cast iron
   C. babbitt   D. carborundum

10. In a motor having sleeve bearings, bearing wear can be checked by measuring the air-gap clearance between the armature and the

    A. pole pieces   B. commutator
    C. bearing   D. brushes

11. If the scale on a shop drawing is 1/4 inch to the foot, then the length of a part which measures 2 3/8 inches long on the drawing is ACTUALLY _____ feet.

    A. 9 1/2   B. 8 1/2   C. 7 1/4   D. 4 1/4

12. When welding cast iron with an oxy-acetylene torch, the BEST weld is obtained when the cast iron is

    A. not preheated
    B. preheated slowly
    C. chilled quickly after welding
    D. chilled slowly after welding

13. A substance which can do the MOST damage to wire rope is

    A. acid   B. grease   C. gasoline   D. oil

14. When comparing the same nominal size of extra strong iron pipe with standard iron pipe, the extra strong iron pipe has _____ diameter _____ diameter.

    A. the same inside; but a larger outside
    B. the same outside; but a smaller inside
    C. a larger outside; and a smaller inside
    D. a larger inside; and a larger outside

15. A *Lally* column which is used in building construction consists of

    A. a large diameter pipe fitted with a base plate at each end
    B. channels tied with lattice bars
    C. unequal sections of round pipe
    D. angles and plates

16. On a 10-24 x 7/8" screw, the number 10 indicates that the size of the outside diameter is MOST NEARLY

    A. 0.187"   B. 10/64"   C. 10/32"   D. 0.10"

17. The liquid solution in an electrical storage battery MOST commonly is

    A. alkali
    B. acid
    C. pure distilled water
    D. copper sulphate

18. Manifolds on an internal combustion engine are used

    A. to mount the engine to the frame
    B. for cooling the engine
    C. in the carburetor
    D. to conduct gases into and out of the engine

19. For winter servicing of a gasoline engine, it is BEST to use an oil that

    A. has a low SAE number
    B. has a high SAE number
    C. has a very heavy consistency
    D. contains few additive detergents

20. To remove a slotted collar having internal threads from a shaft, the BEST of the following wrenches to use is a(n) _____ wrench.

    A. Allen   B. Stillson   C. socket   D. spanner

21. When using a heavy jack placed on the ground to raise a heavy load, it is important to place a sturdy, flat board under the jack PRIMARILY in order to

    A. facilitate placing the jack under the load
    B. reduce the jacking effort
    C. prevent the jack from slipping out from under the load
    D. decrease the jacking height

22. The pulley wheels of a block and tackle are COMMONLY called

    A. stocks   B. swivels   C. sheaves   D. guides

23. If the diameter of a machined part must be 1.035 ± 0.003", then it is ACCEPTABLE if it measures

    A. 1.031"   B. 1.032"   C. 1.039"   D. 1.335"

24. The type of threads for ordinary screws are USUALLY the _____ type.

    A. square   B. buttress   C. V   D. Acme

25. Lead is NORMALLY used in caulking _____ pipe.

    A. copper
    B. brass
    C. steel
    D. cast iron

26. Of the following materials, the one which is COMMONLY used as a lubricant is 26.____

    A. powdered iron oxide B. powdered graphite
    C. casein D. rosin flux

27. On grinders, the tool rest is generally 1/8-inch from the face of the wheel. 27.____
    When dressing small parts on grinders, greater clearance is usually undesirable,
    because too much clearance may cause

    A. the work piece to jam and break the wheel
    B. material from the work piece to be ground off too rapidly
    C. the cutting action of the grinder to be hidden from view
    D. scoring of the wheel

28. The BEST way to determine whether the locknuts on terminals in an electrical terminal 28.____
    box have become loose is to

    A. use an electric tester
    B. try to tighten the nuts with an appropriate wrench
    C. tap the nuts with an insulated handle
    D. try to loosen the nuts with a pair of pliers

29. It is necessary to pour a new concrete floor for a shop. If the dimensions of the concrete 29.____
    slab for the floor are to be 27' x 18' x 6", then the number of cubic yards of concrete that
    must be poured is

    A. 9 B. 16 C. 54 D. 243

30. The jaws of a vise move 1/4" for each complete turn of the handle. 30.____
    The number of complete turns necessary to open the jaws 2 3/4" is

    A. 9 B. 10 C. 11 D. 12

31. The sum of 5'6", 7'3", 9' 3 1/2", and 3' 7 1/4" is 31.____

    A. 19' 8 1/2" B. 22' 1/2" C. 25' 7 3/4" D. 28' 8 3/4"

32. Of the following statements describing the use of carbon dioxide type fire extinguishers, 32.____
    the one which is TRUE is that they

    A. may be used on grease fires
    B. should not be used to extinguish electrical fires
    C. can not be used on most types of fires
    D. are ideal for use in poorly ventilated areas

33. The PRIMARY reason for a twist drill *splitting up the center* is that the 33.____

    A. cutting edges were ground at different angles
    B. lips were ground at different lengths
    C. lip clearance angle was too great
    D. lip clearance angle was insufficient

34. The PROPER file a machinist should use for finishing ordinary flat surfaces is the _____ 34.____
    file.

    A. Pillar B. Warding
    C. Hooktooth D. Hand

35. An all hard saw blade should be used in a hacksaw frame when sawing

   A. tool steel
   B. channel iron
   C. aluminum
   D. thin wall copper tubing

36. The surface gage is generally NOT used for

   A. laying out
   B. leveling and lining up work
   C. checking angles and tapers
   D. locating centers on rough work

Questions 37-40.

DIRECTIONS: The sketch shown below refers to a piping arrangement for connecting a new space heater. Questions 37 through 40 are based on it.

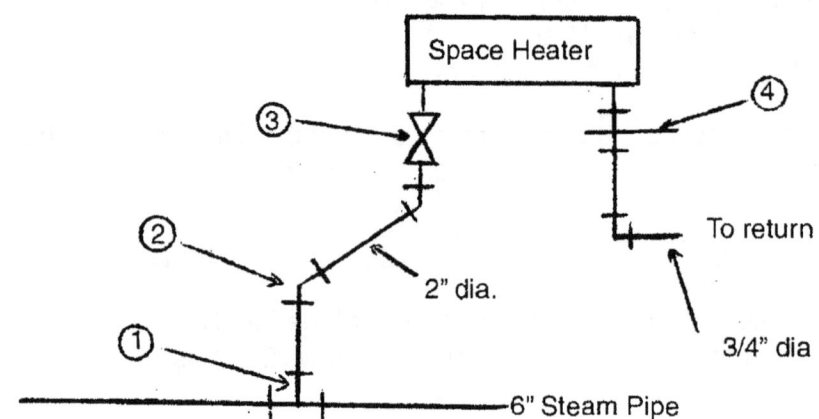

37. Pipe fitting 1 is a

   A. bull tee
   B. sanitary tee
   C. reducing tee
   D. cross

38. Pipe fitting 2 is a

   A. branch tee
   B. Y fitting
   C. right elbow
   D. 45 degree elbow

39. Pipe fitting 3 is a

   A. coupling
   B. flange
   C. valve
   D. steam trap

40. Pipe fitting 4 is a

   A. union   B. valve   C. tee   D. reducer

KEY (CORRECT ANSWERS)

1.	A	11.	A	21.	C	31.	C
2.	D	12.	B	22.	C	32.	A
3.	C	13.	A	23.	B	33.	D
4.	B	14.	B	24.	C	34.	D
5.	C	15.	A	25.	D	35.	A
6.	A	16.	A	26.	B	36.	C
7.	B	17.	B	27.	A	37.	C
8.	D	18.	D	28.	B	38.	D
9.	C	19.	A	29.	A	39.	C
10.	A	20.	D	30.	C	40.	A

MECHANICAL APTITUDE
TOOL RECOGNITION AND USE

EXAMINATION SECTION
TEST 1

DIRECTIONS: Each question or incomplete statement below is followed by several suggested answers or completions. Select the one that *BEST* answers the question or completes the statement.

KEY: CORRECT ANSWERS APPEAR AT THE END OF THIS TEST.

1.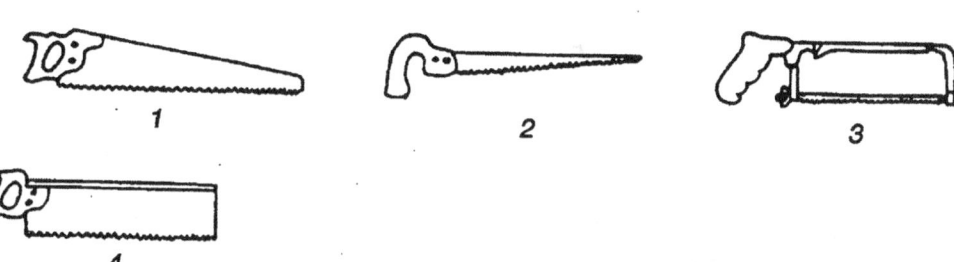

   The saw that is used principally where curved cuts are to be made is numbered

   1. 1   2. 2   3. 3   4. 4

2.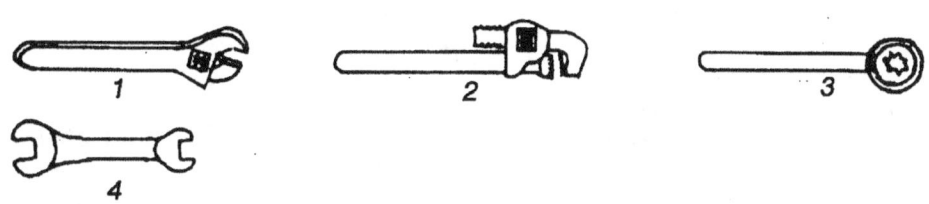

   The wrench that is used principally for pipe work is numbered

   1. 1   2. 2   3. 3   4. 4

3.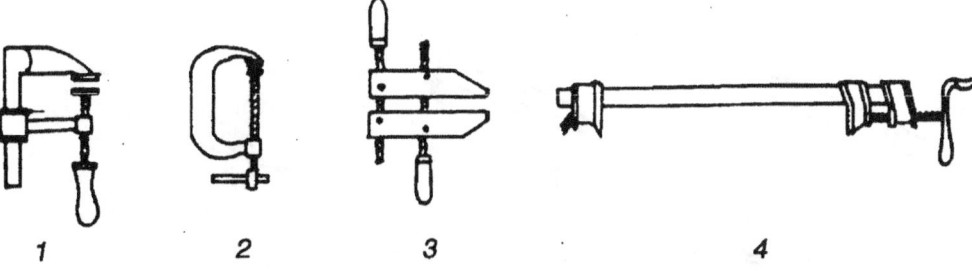

   The carpenter's "hand screw" is numbered

   1. 1   2. 2   3. 3   4. 4

4.

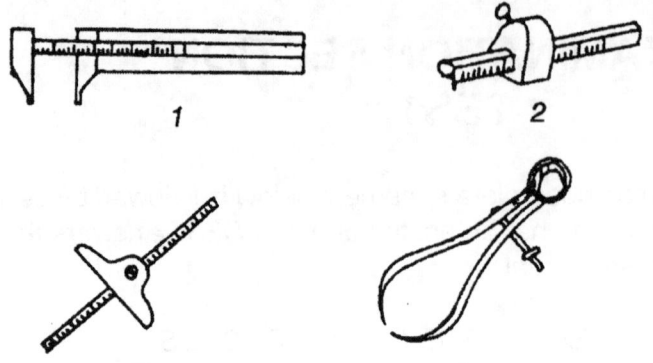

The tool used to measure the depth of a hole is numbered

1. 1 2. 2 3. 3 4. 4

5.

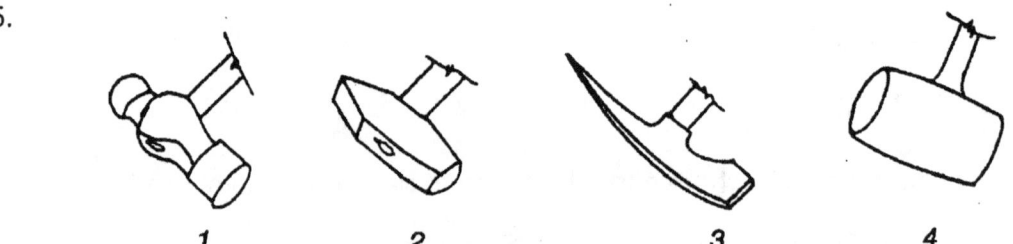

The tool that is best suited for use with a wood chisel is numbered

1. 1 2. 2 3. 3 4. 4

6.

1 *2* *3* *4*

The screw head that would be tightened with an "Allen" wrench is numbered

1. 1 2. 2 3. 3 4. 4

7.

 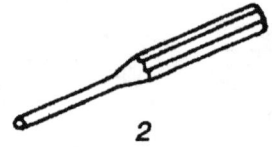 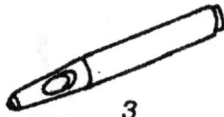

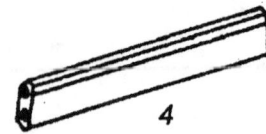

The center punch is numbered

1. 1 2. 2 3. 3 4. 4

8.

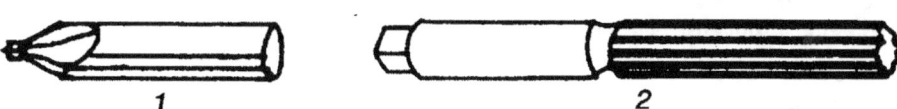

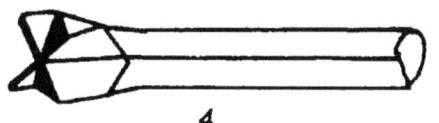

The tool used to drill a hole in concrete is numbered

1. 1 2. 2 3. 3 4. 4

9.

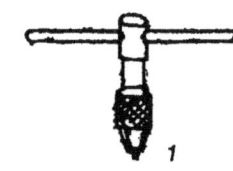
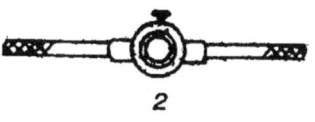

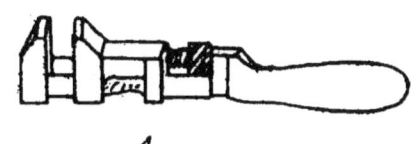

The wrench whose principal purpose is to hold taps for threading is numbered

1. 1 2. 2 3. 3 4. 4

10.

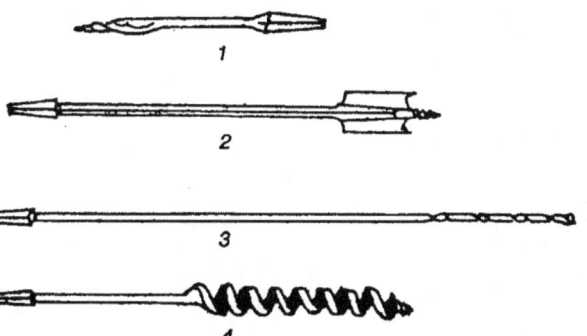

The electrician's bit is indicated by the number

1. 1 2. 2 3. 3 4. 4

11. The head of a cold chisel is "mushroomed" as shown in the sketch. The use of a chisel in this condition is poor practice because
    1. it is impossible to hit the head squarely
    2. the chisel will not cut accurately
    3. chips might fly from the head
    4. the chisel has lost its "temper"

11._____

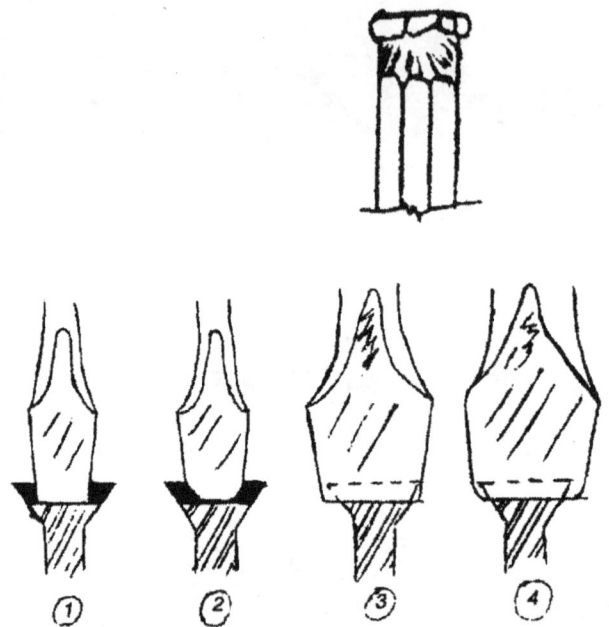

12. The above diagrams show a section of a screw with a screwdriver that is to be used with the screw. The one of the diagrams that shows the correct shape of screwdriver is

12._____

1. 1   2. 2   3. 3   4. 4

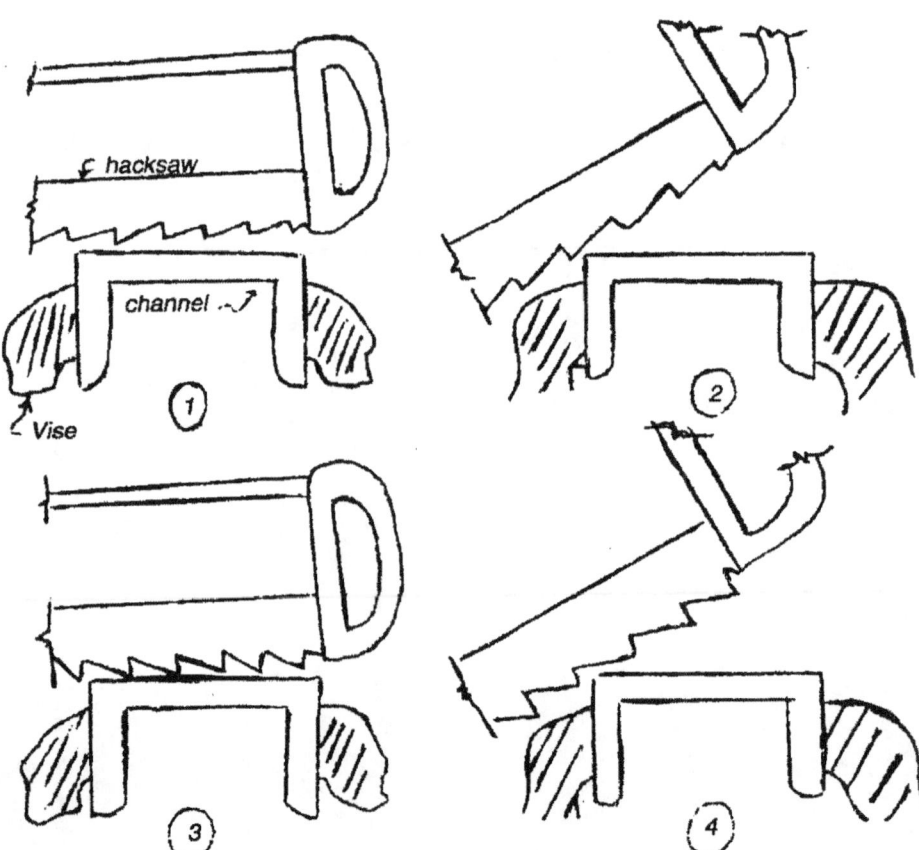

13. A steel channel is to be cut through with a hacksaw. The correct method for doing this is shown in the diagram numbered (diagrams above) 13.____

    1. 1   2. 2   3. 3   4. 4

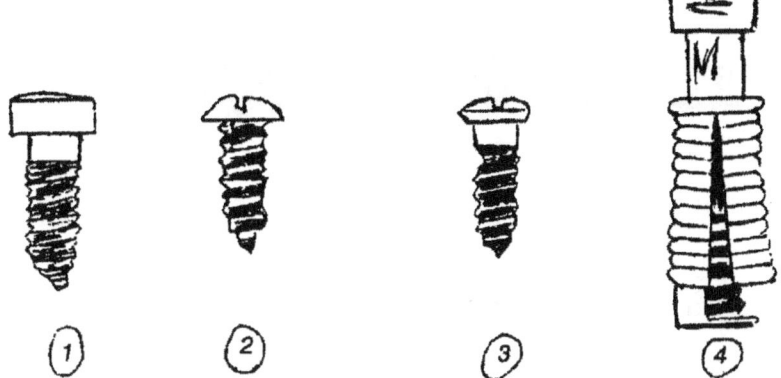

14. The screw above that is most frequently used for sheet metal work is numbered 14.____

    1. 1   2. 2   3. 3   4. 4

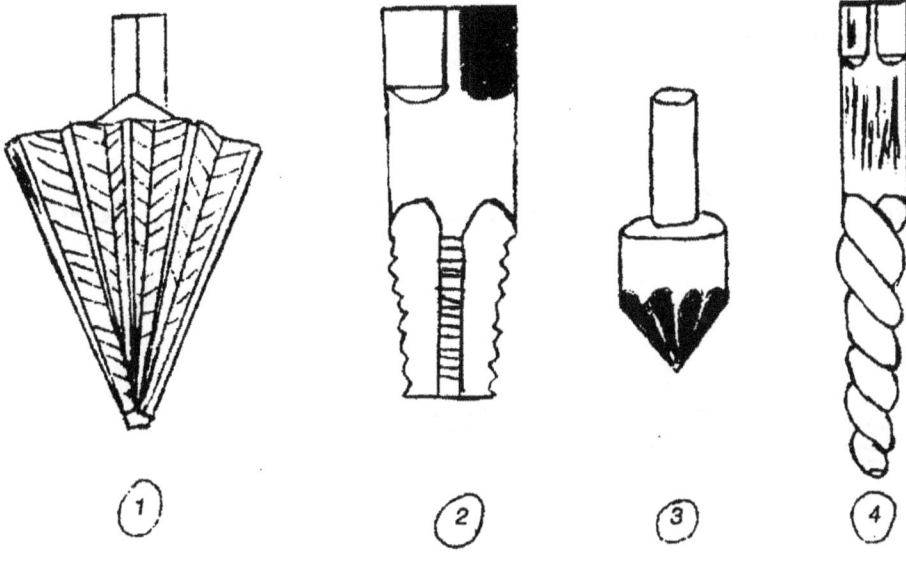

15. The tool used to ream the ends of pipe after the pipe has been cut is shown above in the diagram numbered 15.___

    1. 1   2. 2   3. 3   4. 4

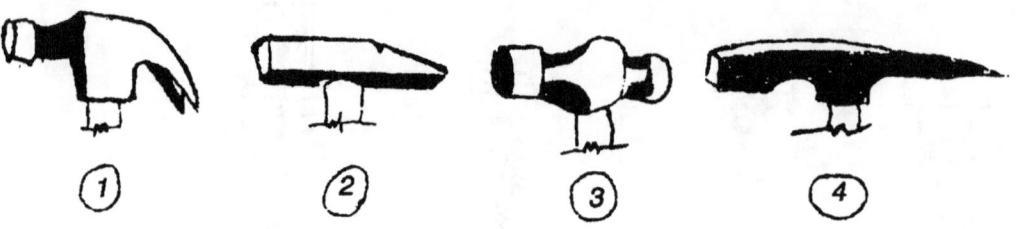

16. The hammer that would be used by a mason to trim brick is shown in the above diagram numbered 16.___

    1. 1   2. 2   3. 3   4. 4

17. The saw intended especially to make accurate miter cuts is shown in the above diagram numbered 17.___

    1. 1   2. 2   3. 3   4. 4

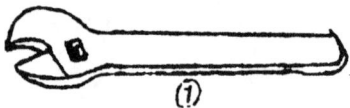 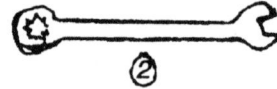
 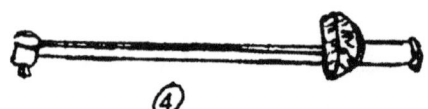

18. A wrench used to tighten cylinder head bolts to a specified torque is shown in the above diagram numbered

   1. 1　　　　2. 2　　　　3. 3　　　　4. 4

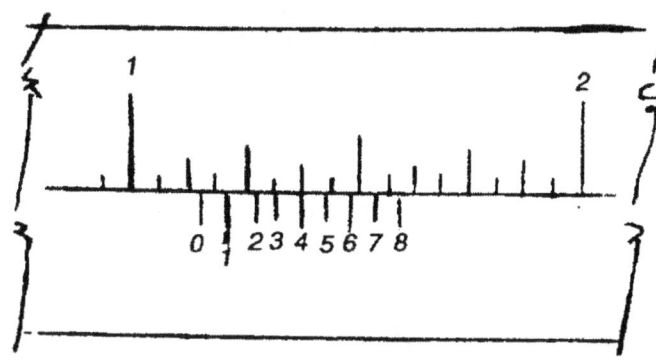

19. A section of the scale of a vernier caliper is shown above. The reading of this caliper setting is most nearly

   1. 1 3/8　　　　2. 1 5/64　　　　3. 1 5/32　　　　4. 1 7/64

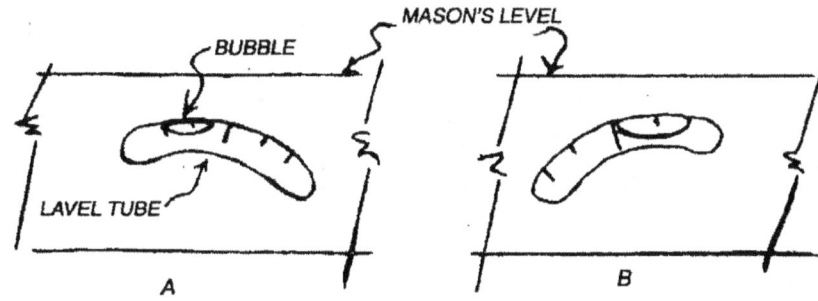

20. A level is placed on a table and the bubble moves to the position indicated in diagram A above. The level is then turned end for end and placed in the same location on the table as before. The bubble now appears as shown in diagram B. The one of the following statements that is correct is

   1. the left end of the table is higher than the right end
   2. the right end of the table is higher than the left end
   3. it is impossible to tell which end of the table is higher
   4. the level tube is not set properly in the level

21. The flat-head screw is No.

   1. 1　　　　2. 2　　　　3. 3　　　　4. 4

  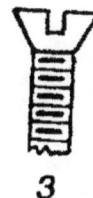 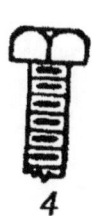

8 (#1)

22. The "Phillips" head is No.

    1. 1   2. 2   3. 3   4. 4

22.___

23. The standard coupling for rigid electrical conduit is

    1. 1   2. 2   3. 3   4. 4

23.___

  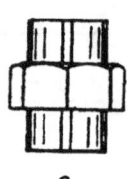 

24. The shape of nut most commonly used on electrical terminals is

    1. 1   2. 2   3. 3   4. 4

24.___

25. The stove bolt is

    1. 1   2. 2   3. 3   4. 4

25.___

KEY (CORRECT ANSWERS)

1.	2	11.	3
2.	2	12.	1
3.	3	13.	1
4.	3	14.	2
5.	4	15.	1
6.	3	16.	4
7.	1	17.	3
8.	4	18.	4
9.	1	19.	3
10.	3	20.	4

21. 3
22. 4
23. 1
24. 2
25. 3

READING COMPREHENSION
UNDERSTANDING AND INTERPRETING WRITTEN MATERIAL
EXAMINATION SECTION
TEST 1

DIRECTIONS: Each question or incomplete statement is followed by several suggested answers or completions. Select the one that BEST answers the question or completes the statement. *PRINT THE LETTER OF THE CORRECT ANSWER IN THE SPACE AT THE RIGHT.*

Questions 1-5.

DIRECTIONS: Questions 1 through 5 are to be answered SOLELY on the basis of the following passage.

Stopping, standing, and parking of motor vehicles is regulated by law to keep the public highways open for a smooth flow of traffic, and to keep stopped vehicles from blocking intersections, driveways, signs, fire hydrants, and other areas that must be kept clear. These established regulations apply in all situations, unless otherwise indicated by signs. Other local restrictions are posted in the areas to which they apply. Three examples of these other types of restrictions, which may apply singly or in combination with one another, are:

NO STOPPING: This means that a driver may not stop a vehicle for any purpose except when necessary to avoid interference with other vehicles, or in compliance with directions of a police officer or signal.

NO STANDING: This means that a driver may stop a vehicle only temporarily to actually receive or discharge passengers.

NO PARKING: This means that a driver may stop a vehicle only temporarily to actually load or unload merchandise or passengers. When stopped, it is advisable to turn on warning flashers if equipped with them. However, one should never use a directional signal for this purpose, because it may confuse the other drivers. Some NO PARKING signs prohibit parking between certain hours on certain days. For example, the sign may read NO PARKING 8 A.M. TO 11 A.M. MONDAY, WEDNESDAY, FRIDAY. These signs are usually utilized on streets where cleaning operations take place on alternate days.

1. The parking regulation that applies to fire hydrants is an example of _____ regulations.
   A. local   B. established   C. posted   D. temporary

   1._____

2. When stopped in a NO PARKING zone, it is ADVISABLE to
   A. turn on the right directional signal to indicate to other drivers that you will remain stopped
   B. turn on the left directional signal to indicate to other drivers that you may be leaving the curb after a period of time

   2._____

C. turn on the warning flashers if your car is equipped with them
D. put the vehicle in reverse so that the backup lights will be on to warn approaching cars that you have temporarily stopped

3. You may stop a vehicle temporarily to discharge passengers in an area under the restriction of a _____ zone.
   A. NO STOPPING – NO STANDING
   B. NO STANDING – NO PARKING
   C. NO PARKING – NO STOPPING
   D. NO STOPPING – NO STANDING – NO PARKING

4. A sign reads NO PARKING 8 A.M. TO 11 A.M., MONDAY, WEDNESDAY, FRIDAY.
   Based on this sign, a parking enforcement agent would issue a summons to a car that is parked on a _____ at _____ A.M.
   A. Tuesday; 9:30
   B. Wednesday; 12:00
   C. Friday; 10:30
   D. Saturday; 8:00

5. NO PARKING signs prohibiting parking between certain hours, on certain days, are USUALLY utilized on streets where
   A. vehicles frequently take on and discharge passengers
   B. cleaning operations take place on alternate days
   C. NO STOPPING signs have been ignored
   D. commercial vehicles take on and unload merchandise

Questions 6-15.

DIRECTIONS: Questions 6 through 15 are to be answered SOLELY on the basis of the following passage.

Parking Enforcement Agents in Iron City work three shifts. The first shift is from 10 A.M. to 6 P.M. The second shift is from 6 P.M. to 2 A.M. The third shift is from 2 A.M. to 10 A.M. Each shift at the Central Office employs three people who patrol the surrounding area. Parking Enforcement Agents have one hour off per shift for lunch.

Starting on Tuesday, Agents Fred Black, Mary Evans, and Thomas Hart worked the first shift. Harold Wilson and Mary Wood worked the second shift. The third agent for the second shift was ill. Thomas Hart worked the second shift in addition to his regular first shift, and thus earned overtime pay. Mike Brown, Anne Hill, and Jeff Smith worked the third shift.

On his first shift, Agent Thomas Hart wrote 11 summonses for meter violations, 15 summonses for double parking, and 13 summonses for parking in a no-standing zone. On his second shift, Thomas Hart wrote 21 summonses for double parking, 13 summonses for meter violations, and 15 summonses for parking in a no-standing zone.

6. On Tuesday, Agent Mary Wood was on duty from
   A. 6 A.M. to 2 P.M.
   B. 10 A.M. to 6 P.M.
   C. 2 A.M. to 6 P.M.
   D. 6 P.M. to 2 A.M.

7. How many Parking Enforcement Agents normally work from 6 P.M. to 2 A.M.? 7.____
   A. One B. Two C. Three D. Four

8. The number of Parking Enforcement Agents who ACTUALLY worked the 8.____
   second shift on Tuesday was
   A. one B. two C. three D. four

9. Among the three successive shifts which started on Tuesday, the total 9.____
   number of DIFFERENT Parking Enforcement Agents who actually reported for
   duty was
   A. 7 B. 8 C. 9 D. 10

10. The total number of summonses Agent Hart wrote during the FIRST shift 10.____
    he worked was
    A. 11 B. 13 C. 39 D. 49

11. Agent Hill was scheduled to finish her shift at 11.____
    A. 10 A.M. B. 6 P.M. C. 10 P.M. D. 2 A.M.

12. Parking Enforcement Agents have one hour off per shift. The TOTAL hours 12.____
    actually worked by Agent Evans on Tuesday was _____ hours.
    A. 8 B. 7½ C. 7 D. 6½

13. The TOTAL number of summonses Agent Hart wrote for meter violations was 13.____
    A. 15 B. 24 C. 26 D. 34

14. During both his shifts, Agent Hart wrote the MOST summonses for 14.____
    A. meter violations   B. standing in a no-parking zone
    C. double parking   D. parking in a no-standing zone

15. The TOTAL number of summonses Agent Hart wrote during his two shifts was 15.____
    A. 28 B. 48 C. 68 D. 88

Questions 16-22.

DIRECTIONS: Questions 16 through 22 are to be answered SOLELY on the basis of the following passage.

The parking meter was designed 30 years ago primarily as a mechanism to assist in reducing overtime parking at the curb, to increase parking turnover, and to facilitate enforcement of parking regulations. That the meter has accomplished these basic functions is attested to by its use in an increasing number of cities.

A recent survey of cities in the United States indicates that overtime parking was reduced 75% or more in 47% of the cities surveyed, and to a lesser degree in 43% of the cities surveyed, making a total of 90% of the cities surveyed where the parking meter was found to be effective in reducing overtime parking at the curb.

A side effect of the reduction in overtime parking is the increase in parking turnover. Approximately 89% of the places surveyed found meters useful in this respect. Meters also encourage even spacing of cars at the curb. Unmetered curb parking is often so irregular that it wastes space or makes parking and departure difficult.

The effectiveness of parking meters, in the final analysis, rests upon the enforcement of regulations by squads of enforcement agents who will diligently patrol the metered area. The task of checking parking time is made easier with meters, since violations can be checked from a moving vehicle or by visual sightings of an agent on foot patrol, and the laborious process of chalking tires is greatly reduced. It is reported that, after meters have been installed, it takes on the average only 25% of the time formerly required to patrol the same area.

The fact that a parker activates a mechanism that immediately begins to count time, that will indicate exactly when the parking time has expired, and that will advertise such fact by showing a red flag, tends to make a parker more conscious of his parking responsibilities than the hit and miss system of possible detection by a patrolman.

16. According to the above passage, when the parking meter was introduced, one of its major purposes was NOT to
   A. cut down overtime curb parking
   B. make curb parking available to more parkers
   C. bring in revenue from parking fees
   D. make it easier to enforce parking regulations

17. In the cities surveyed, how effective was the installation of parking meters in cutting down overtime parking?
   A. It was effective to some degree in all of the cities surveyed.
   B. It was ineffective in only one out of every ten cities surveyed.
   C. It reduced overtime parking at least 75% in most cities surveyed.
   D. There was only a small reduction in overtime parking in 43% of the cities surveyed.

18. When overtime parking is reduced by the installation of parking meters, an accompanying result is
   A. an increase in the amount of parking space
   B. the use of the available parking spaces by more cars
   C. the faster movement of traffic
   D. a decrease in the number of squads required to enforce traffic regulations

19. According to the above passage, on streets which have parking meters, as compared with streets which are unmetered,
   A. there is less waste of parking space
   B. parking is more difficult
   C. parking time limits are irregular
   D. drivers waste more time looking for an empty parking space

20. According to the above passage, the use of parking meters will NOT be effective unless
    A. parking areas are patrolled in automobiles
    B. it is combined with the chalking of tires
    C. the public cooperates
    D. there is strict enforcement of parking regulations

21. According to the above passage, one reason why there is greater compliance with parking regulations when parking time is regulated by meters rather than by a foot patrolman chalking tires is that
    A. overtime parking becomes glaringly evident to everyone
    B. the parker is himself responsible for operating the timing mechanism
    C. there is no personal relationship between parker and enforcing officer
    D. the timing of elapsed parking time is accurate

22. In the last paragraph of the above passage, the words *a parker activates a mechanism* refers to the fact that a motorist
    A. starts the timing device of the meter working
    B. parks his car
    C. checks whether the meter is working
    D. starts the engine of his car

Questions 23-25.

DIRECTIONS: Questions 6 through 15 are to be answered SOLELY on the basis of the information given in the following passage.

When markings upon the curb or the pavement of a street designate parking space, no person shall stand or park a vehicle in such designated parking space so that any part of such vehicle occupies more than one such space or protrudes beyond the markings designating such a space, except that a vehicle which is a size too large to be parked within a single designated parking space shall be parked with the front bumper at the front of the space with the rear of the vehicle extending as little as possible into the adjoining space to the rear, or vice-versa.

23. The regulation quoted above applies to parking at any
    A. curb or pavement
    B. metered spaces
    C. street where parking is permitted
    D. parking spaces with marked boundaries

24. The regulation quoted above prohibits the occupying of more than one indicated parking space by
    A. any vehicle
    B. large vehicles
    C. small vehicles
    D. vehicles in spaces partially occupied

25. In the regulation quoted above, the term *vice-versa* refers to a vehicle of a size too large parked with
    A. front bumper flush with front of parking space it occupies
    B. front of vehicle extending into front of parking space
    C. rear bumper flush with rear of parking space it occupies
    D. rear of vehicle protruding into adjoining parking space

KEY (CORRECT ANSWERS)

1.	B	11.	A
2.	C	12.	C
3.	B	13.	B
4.	C	14.	C
5.	B	15.	D
6.	D	16.	C
7.	C	17.	B
8.	C	18.	B
9.	B	19.	A
10.	C	20.	D

21.	A
22.	A
23.	D
24.	C
25.	C

TEST 2

DIRECTIONS: Each question or incomplete statement is followed by several suggested answers or completions. Select the one that BEST answers the question or completes the statement. *PRINT THE LETTER OF THE CORRECT ANSWER IN THE SPACE AT THE RIGHT.*

Questions 1-5.

DIRECTIONS: Questions 1 through 5 are to be answered SOLELY on the basis of the following bulletin on SCHOOL ELIGIBILITY CARDS.

SCHOOL ELIGIBILITY CARDS

All bus operators are responsible for the proper use of School Eligibility Cards for reduced fares on their buses. These cards are issued to elementary and high school students. Such cards are good for the entire year from September 13 to June 28, and are issued subject to the following conditions:

- A. The card is to be used by the student whose name appears on the face of the card, and only on days when school is in session. If offered by any other person, it will be taken away by the bus operator, and full fare will be collected from the person presenting the card.
- B. The card will allow the student to ride on the particular bus indicated on the face of the card for a fare of fifty cents between 6 A.M. and 7 P.M. The fare of 50 cents must be deposited in the fare box by the student after the card is shown to the bus operator.
- C. The student, after paying the 50 cent fare, is entitled to the same transfer privileges as other passengers.
- D. The card will be taken away if altered or misused, and the student will not be given a new card for a period of five school months.
- E. The card is not good unless all entries on the card are made by the teacher and the card is signed by the teacher.

1. If a student's School Eligibility Card is taken away by a bus operator because of misuse, the student will
   - A. never be issued a new card because of this misuse
   - B. not be issued a new card until he pays for the old one
   - C. be eligible for a new card after five school months
   - D. be eligible for a new card if he gets a note from his teacher

   1.____

2. A bus operator should take away a School Eligibility Card if it is presented
   - A. at 9 A.M. before school opens
   - B. at 3 P.M. after school opens
   - C. by a college student
   - D. more than twice a day

   2.____

3. A bus operator should permit a student to ride at reduced fare if he presents his School Eligibility Card at
   - A. 8:00 A.M. on Sunday
   - B. 8 A.M. on Monday
   - C. 8:00 A.M. on Saturday
   - D. 8:00 P.M. on Wednesday

   3.____

4. If a student presents a School Eligibility Card, pays a 50 cent fare, and asks for a transfer, the bus operator should
   A. tell the student that during school hours he may not get a transfer
   B. tell him to use his School Eligibility Card instead
   C. give him a transfer if other passengers can get them free
   D. tell him he must pay the full dollar fare to get one

5. According to the above bulletin, School Eligibility Cards are NOT good on
   A. September 15   B. October 26
   C. February 23   D. June 30

Questions 6-12.

DIRECTIONS: Questions 6 through 12 are to be answered SOLELY on the basis of the following passage on the EXTRACT OF RULES FOR SYSTEM PICK FOR BUS OPERATORS.

EXTRACT OF RULES FOR SYSTEM PICK FOR BUS OPERATORS

Operators picking up an early run (one ending before 9:00 P.M., including all time allowances) on weekdays must pick an early run on Saturday and Sunday.

No operator will be allowed to pick on the extra list unless he desires to transfer to a depot where all runs, tricks, etc. have been picked.

After an operator finishes picking and the monitor has entered the operator's name for the run on the picking board, no change of run will be permitted. Erasures and other signs of mutilation will not be permitted on the picking board.

It is planned to permit about 100 operators in the picking room at one time, but the time allowed for any one person to pick will not exceed five minutes. If for any reason you cannot attend, you may submit a preference slip or be represented by proxy.

An operator inactive because of sickness, injury, etc. for sixty days prior to his pick assignment must present a certificate from a doctor stating he may return to duty not later than two weeks after date of pick.

Your cooperation is requested. Please be on hand to pick at your designated time, and leave picking room promptly when you have finished picking.

6. The rules apply to a pick of
   A. Saturday and Sunday   B. depot extra
   C. weekday   D. system

7. An operator picking an early run on weekdays
   A. cannot be off on Saturdays or Sundays
   B. must submit a preference slip
   C. will be assigned to the extra list on other days
   D. must pick an early run on Saturday and Sunday

8. According to the rules, an operator
   A. will be in the picking room alone while designating his choice
   B. must wait in the picking room after making his choice until all runs have been chosen
   C. is informed that he may pick his run at any time he wishes to on pick day
   D. may have someone else pick for him if he cannot be present on the day of the pick

9. In order to pick on the extra list, an operator MUST
   A. present a doctor's certificate
   B. have been inactive for sixty days
   C. appear at the picking room in person
   D. be willing to transfer to a terminal where all the runs have been picked

10. Once a bus operator picks a run and his name has been entered by the monitor, he
    A. must accept the run picked as no changes will be permitted
    B. can change his mind if the choice was made by proxy
    C. may ask the monitor to erase his pick if the next man has not yet picked
    D. can swap runs with another operator but only after sixty days

11. An operator making his pick after having been out sick for three months must
    A. pick on the extra list
    B. present a doctor's certificate to the monitor
    C. wait two weeks before returning to duty
    D. pick an early run or trick

12. The rules state that
    A. only 100 operators can pick in any one day
    B. cooperation is demanded, and a penalty will be imposed on any operator who is uncooperative
    C. a preference slip must be signed by the monitor
    D. an operator must make his pick within 5 minutes time

Questions 13-20.

DIRECTIONS: Questions 13 through 20 are to be answered SOLELY on the basis of the following passage on LOST PROPERTY.

LOST PROPERTY

When a passenger turns over a piece of lost property to a porter, or when a porter finds a lost article, he shall turn it in to the most convenient office equipped with a Lost Property bag and shall obtain a receipt therefor from the employee responsible for handling lost property. The responsible employee must forward articles of great value, such as expensive jewelry or large sums of money, to the Lost Property Office by special messenger as soon as possible and notify the Desk Trainmaster. The responsible employee must turn over all firearms to the Transit Police, take a proper receipt, and notify the Lost Property Office as soon as possible.

Perishable property, such as food products not in cans or boxes and requiring refrigeration, should be sold at the terminal by the terminal supervisor after holding for 8 hours, and the money forwarded to the Administrative Office; if the property is not sold, it should be destroyed and a record made on the lost property form.

13. A porter MUST turn over a lost umbrella at the _____ office.
    A. desk trainmaster's
    B. lost property
    C. transit police
    D. most convenient

14. A porter who finds a pistol on a station should take it to the _____ office.
    A. transit police
    B. lost property
    C. administrative
    D. most convenient

15. The Lost Property Office is mentioned
    A. once   B. twice   C. three times   D. four times

16. If a porter finds a carton of canned peas, he should
    A. sell it   B. destroy it   C. keep it   D. turn it in

17. If a porter finds a burlap bag containing about 15 pounds of fresh fish, he should
    A. sell it   B. destroy it   C. keep it   D. turn it in

18. A porter must get a receipt for a lost article to prove that he
    A. found it
    B. received it
    C. turned it in
    D. knows what it is

19. A special messenger is NOT required to be used for a
    A. bag of 10 dollar bills
    B. silver-handled pistol
    C. gold candlestick
    D. genuine pearl necklace

20. A porter finding a box of flowers with a tag showing the addressee should
    A. deliver it
    B. turn it in
    C. telephone addressee
    D. take it to the Lost Property Office

Questions 21-25.

DIRECTIONS: Questions 21 through 25 are to be answered SOLELY on the basis of the following passage on BUS RADIO TRANSMISSION CODE.

BUS RADIO TRANSMISSION CODE

Buses are equipped with a 2-way radio system to aid the bus operator in the performance of his job. It is used primarily to transmit information to the Radio Dispatcher located in the Central Radio Operations Center. To assist the bus operator in the transmission of information without loss of time or possible confusion, the following Code is used:

Code Red Tag: To be used only in extreme emergency, such as police assistance in the event of a hold-up, assault, serious vandalism, etc. The bus operator transmitting a Red Tag Alert shall have priority over all other incoming calls. All other bus operators shall stand by until Dispatcher gives order to resume normal operations.
Code 1: Collision involving a bus.
Code 2: Passenger injured on board bus.
Code 3: Disabled bus.
Code 4: Bus blocked by fire apparatus, other vehicle, parade, etc.

21. If a bus operator observes a mugging taking place on his bus, he should radio a Code
    A. 1   B. 2   C. 3   D. 4

22. If a passenger trips and hurts himself on a bus, the bus operator should radio a Code
    A. 1   B. 2   C. 3   D. 4

23. If a bus is blocked by a street demonstration of marching adults, the bus operator should radio a Code
    A. 1   B. 2   C. 4   D. Red Tag

24. While a bus operator is reporting an injury to a passenger who fell and hurt his leg on the bus, a second bus operator interrupts this radio conversation with a Code Red Tag.
    The FIRST bus operator should
    A. continue with his message so that the passenger may be aided quickly
    B. repeat his message since the interruption may have scrambled his voice
    C. immediately stop talking
    D. ask the second bus operator to wait until he has completed his message

25. If a bus engine stalls and cannot be restarted, the bus operator should radio a Code
    A. 1   B. 2   C. 3   D. Red Tag

KEY (CORRECT ANSWERS)

1.	C	11.	B
2.	C	12.	D
3.	B	13.	D
4.	C	14.	D
5.	D	15.	B
6.	D	16.	D
7.	D	17.	D
8.	D	18.	C
9.	D	19.	B
10.	A	20.	B

21.	D
22.	B
23.	C
24.	C
25.	C

ARITHMETICAL REASONING
EXAMINATION SECTION
TEST 1

DIRECTIONS: Each question or incomplete statement is followed by several suggested answers or completions. Select the one that BEST answers the question or completes the statement. *PRINT THE LETTER OF THE CORRECT ANSWER IN THE SPACE AT THE RIGHT.*

1. At a certain city garage, there are 216 cars. Of these, 1/2 are assigned to Department P, 1/3 to Department Q, 1/9 to Department R, and the rest to Department S. How many cars are assigned to Department S?

    A. 9   B. 12   C. 18   D. 24

    1._____

2. In August a car travels 572 miles; in September, 438 miles; in October, 898 miles; and in December it travels 609 miles.
   If the five month average from August through December was 673 miles traveled a month, then the number of miles traveled in November was

    A. 638   B. 706   C. 774   D. 848

    2._____

3. Suppose the Units R, S, and T gave out a total of 1,715 parking tickets.
   If Unit R gave out twice as many tickets as Unit S, and Unit T gave out twice as many tickets as Unit R, the number of tickets given out by Unit S is

    A. 270   B. 255   C. 245   D. 225

    3._____

4. A car travels at the average rate of 40 miles an hour on the highway.
   If it takes 5 hours to make a trip of 150 miles, 2/3 of which is on the highway and the rest on city streets, what was the AVERAGE rate of speed of the car on city streets?

    A. 20   B. 25   C. 30   D. 35

    4._____

5. A motorist uses 27 gallons of gas on a trip of 351 miles. How many gallons of gas would he use if he took a trip of 624 miles under the same condition?

    A. 45   B. 46   C. 47   D. 48

    5._____

6. If the taxi rate in the city is 35 for the first 1/5 of a mile and 5 for each additional 1/5 of a mile, how far did a passenger travel whose fare was 95¢?
   _____ miles.

    A. 2 1/5   B. 2 3/5   C. 3 2/5   D. 3 4/5

    6._____

7. If you drove a car for three-quarters of an hour and kept it at a steady speed of 30 miles per hour for half an hour and a steady speed of 40 miles per hour the rest of the time, you would have traveled _____ miles.

    A. 20   B. 25   C. 30   D. 35

    7._____

8. The length of curb available for the parking of cars on a certain street is 435 feet on the south side and 405 feet on the north side.
Assuming that the bumper-to-bumper length of the average car to be parked is 15 feet, the TOTAL number of cars that can be parked bumper-to-bumper on both sides of the street will be

   A. 56 B. 58 C. 60 D. 61

9. If the charges against a certain vehicle total $2,000 a year, and 7 1/2% of this is for repairs and maintenance, then the annual cost of repairs and maintenance for that vehicle is

   A. $50 B. $100 C. $150 D. $300

10. A 210 foot by 120 foot parking lot is reduced in size by construction of a 36 foot by 54 foot building at one of its corners.
The area left for parking is MOST NEARLY _____ square yards.

    A. 1,800 B. 2,600 C. 22,800 D. 23,300

11. A dispatcher works a total of 44 hours, spending 17 on Special Project A, 13 on Special Project B, and the rest on his usual duties.
The percentage of time he spends on the two special projects is MOST NEARLY

    A. 68% B. 69% C. 70% D. 71%

12. A driver, dispatched from the garage at 8:15 A.M., arrived at his first destination 35 minutes later. He waited 50 minutes at this location before he could go on to his next destination. It took him one hour and 40 minutes traveling time to get to this second location. He then took an hour lunch period before driving back to the garage, a trip that took 45 minutes.
What time did the driver return to the garage?

    A. 12:25 P.M. B. 12:45 P.M.
    C. 1:05 P.M.   D. 1:25 P.M.

13. Truck A has been driven 38,742.3 miles, Truck B has been driven 24,169.7 miles, Truck C has been driven 41,286.4 miles, Truck D has been driven 15,053.5 miles, and Truck E has been driven 8,407.0 miles.
The total mileage of these five trucks combined is MOST NEARLY _____ miles.

    A. 127,650 B. 127,660 C. 128,650 D. 128,660

14. Suppose that the trucks in a certain garage used a total of 86,314 gallons of gas in 1991 and 8,732 gallons less in 1992.
If they used a total of 72,483 gallons of gas in 1993, how much LESS gas was used in 1993 than in 1992?
_____ gallons.

    A. 5,099 B. 5,109 C. 5,199 D. 5,209

15. A driver averaged 17 miles for each gallon of gas used one week and 26 miles the next week.
If he used 38.9 gallons during the first week and 27.6 during the second, the TOTAL number of miles he drove in these two weeks was

    A. 1,266.3 B. 1,322.6 C. 1,378.9 D. 1,435.2

16. In Garage A, 87 drivers worked a total of 427 hours overtime. In Garage B, 53 drivers worked a total of 245 hours overtime.
    Compared to the average overtime worked per man in Garage B, the average overtime worked per man in Garage A was MOST NEARLY _____ of an hour _____.

    A. 2/10; more
    B. 2/10; less
    C. 3/10; more
    D. 3/10; less

17. The scale on a map indicates that every 1 5/8 inches on the map represents 5 miles. If two locations are 13 inches apart on the map, what is the distance between them in miles?

    A. 30
    B. 35
    C. 40
    D. 45

18. The number of yards in a mile is

    A. 5,280
    B. 1,760
    C. 880
    D. 440

19. Add the following numbers: 17 1/2, 29 1/2, and 6 1/2. The CORRECT total is

    A. 32
    B. 42
    C. 53 1/2
    D. 96 1/2

20. Add 1,516 and 3,497; then subtract 766.
    The CORRECT answer is

    A. 2,731
    B. 4,247
    C. 5,357
    D. 5,779

21. Add 39, 24, and 36. Then divide the total by 3.
    The CORRECT answer is

    A. 23
    B. 33
    C. 96
    D. 99

22. A certain paint can cover 310 square feet per gallon. The number of gallons of this paint required to paint 200 lines each 6 inches wide and 18 feet 6 inches long is MOST NEARLY

    A. 2
    B. 4
    C. 6
    D. 8

23. A white paint that can cover 500 square feet of surface per gallon is used to paint the crosswalks at street intersections.
    If the area at each intersection is equal to 300 square feet, the number of gallons required to paint 50 intersections is

    A. 10
    B. 20
    C. 30
    D. 40

24. The dimension 45" expressed in feet is

    A. 3 1/3
    B. 3 1/2
    C. 3 3/4
    D. 3 7/8

25. 85 percent of $5,250 is

    A. $3,463.50
    B. $4,361.50
    C. $4,462.50
    D. $4,666.50

KEY (CORRECT ANSWERS)

1.	B	11.	A
2.	D	12.	C
3.	C	13.	B
4.	A	14.	A
5.	D	15.	C
6.	B	16.	C
7.	B	17.	C
8.	A	18.	B
9.	C	19.	C
10.	B	20.	B

21. B
22. C
23. C
24. C
25. C

———

SOLUTIONS TO PROBLEMS

1. $(1 - 1/2 - 1/3 - 1/9)(216) = 12$ cars

2. Let x = miles traveled in November. Then, $(572+438+898+x+609)/5 = 673$. Solving, $x = 848$

3. Let 2x, x, 4x = number of tickets respectively issued by R, S, T. Then, $2x + x + 4x = 1715$. Solving, $x = 245$

4. Let x = speed on city streets. Then, $\dfrac{100}{40} + \dfrac{50}{x} = 5$ Simplifying, $100x + 2000 = 200x$. Solving, $x = 20$ mph.

5. $351 \div 27 = 13$ miles per gallon. Then, $624 \div 13 = 48$ gallons

6. Let x = number of miles. Then, $.35 + .25(x - 1/5) = .95$ Solving, $x = 2\ 3/5$

7. $(30 \times .50) + (40 \times .25) = 25$ miles

8. $(435+405)/15 = 56$ cars

9. Annual cost of repairs and maintenance = $(.075)(\$2000) = \$150$

10. Area left = $(210')(120') - (36')(54) = 23,256$ sq.ft., closest to 23,300 sq.ft. $\approx 23,300 \div 9 \approx 2600$ sq.yds.

11. $(13+17)/44 = 68.\overline{18}\% \approx 68\%$

12. 8:15 AM + 35 min. + 50 min. + 1 hr. 40 min. + 1 hr. + 45 min. = 8:15 AM + 4 hrs. 50 min. = 1:05 PM

13. $38,742.3 + 24,169.7 + 41,286.4 + 15,053.5 + 8407.0 = 127,658.9 \approx 127,660$ miles

14. $86,314 - 8732 - 72,483 = 5099$ gallons less

15. $(38.9)(17) + (27.6)(26) = 1378.9$ miles

16. Garage A: $427/87 \approx 4.9$ Garage B: $245/53 \approx 4.6$
    So, average overtime was 3/10 of an hour more in Garage A

17. $13 \div 1\ 5/8 = 8$. Then, $(8 \times 5) = 40$ miles

18. 1 mile = $5280 \div 3 = 1760$ yds.

19. $17\ 1/2 + 29\ 1/2 + 6\ 1/2 = 53\ 1/2$

20. $1516 + 3497 - 766 = 4247$

21. $(39+24+36) \div 3 = 99 \div 3 = 33$

22. $(200)(1/2')(18\ 1/2') = 1850$ sq.ft. Then, $1850 \div 310 \approx 6$ gallons

23. $(50)(300\text{ sq.ft.}) = 15,000$ sq.ft. Then, $15,000 \div 500 = 30$ gallons

24. $45" = 45/12 = 3\ 3/4$ ft.

25. $(\$5250)(.85) = \$4462.50$

TEST 2

DIRECTIONS: Each question or incomplete statement is followed by several suggested answers or completions. Select the one that BEST answers the question or completes the statement. *PRINT THE LETTER OF THE CORRECT ANSWER IN THE SPACE AT THE RIGHT.*

1. A vehicle which averages 14 1/2 miles to a gallon of gas uses a quart of oil for every 2 1/2 gallons of gas.
   If the vehicle traveled 19,952 miles in a year, its oil consumption for the year would be _____ quarts.

   A. 52   B. 56   C. 60   D. 64   1._____

2. Thirteen percent of all the vehicles in a certain garage are trucks.
   If there are 26 trucks, then the number of vehicles of other types in this garage is

   A. 174   B. 200   C. 260   D. 338   2._____

3. Of 12 employees in a garage, four earn $35,000 a year, two earn $31,500 a year, one earns $45,500 a year, and the rest each earn $38,000 a year.
   The average yearly salary of these employees is CLOSEST to

   A. $35,500   B. $36,500   C. $37,500   D. $38,500   3._____

4. A garage bin used for storing supplies and parts measures 1 yard x 2 yards x 7 feet.
   The cubic volume of this bin is

   A. 5 1/3 cubic yards   B. 16 cubic feet   4._____
   C. 63 cubic feet   D. 126 cubic feet

5. A garage has a gas tank with a capacity of 1,300 gallons. If there are only 520 gallons of gas in the tank, then the tank is _____ full.

   A. 40%   B. 33 1/3%   C. 25%   D. 16 3/4%   5._____

6. Of a specially selected group of vehicles, 1/5 are 6 months old, 2/5 are 12 months old, and 2/5 are 15 months old.
   The average age of this group of vehicles is _____ months.

   A. 9   B. 10   C. 11   D. 12   6._____

7. A section of a garage used for parking vehicles measures 162 1/2' x 25 3/4'.
   If each vehicle to be parked in this section requires on the average 84 sq. ft. of parking space, the MAXIMUM number of vehicles that can be parked in this section is CLOSEST to

   A. 50   B. 45   C. 40   D. 35   7._____

8. Each of the 23 vehicles in a garage uses an average of 114 gallons of gas every 4 weeks.
   If the motor vehicle dispatcher is required to re-order gas when the gas tank in the garage shows no more than a one week supply, he MUST re-order when the gas tank shows _____ gallons.

   A. 655   B. 705   C. 830   D. 960   8._____

104

9. An employee's annual salary is $45,800. His total annual deductions are 22% for withholding tax, 8% for pension and social security, and $1,820 for health insurance. The take-home pay that this employee would get on the check he receives every other week is MOST NEARLY

   A. $577.10   B. $845.00   C. $1,154.20   D. $1,220.40

10. The list price of truck A is $12,500 and that of truck B is $12,000.
    If the discount on truck A is 20% and the discount on truck B is 10%, how much cheaper would it be to buy truck A instead of truck B?

    A. $800   B. $450   C. $400   D. No cheaper

11. There are three garages located in a single block. Garage A has 3/4 of the capacity of garage B and 2/3 of the capacity of garage C.
    If 88 cars can be parked in garage B, the TOTAL number of cars that can be parked in all of the three garages is

    A. 186   B. 205   C. 238   D. 253

12. The city purchases 5 vehicles costing $6,000 each, 3 vehicles costing $8,000 each, and 2 vehicles costing $13,000 each.
    The TOTAL cost of these vehicles is

    A. $67,000   B. $26,000   C. $80,000   D. $84,000

13. A car that averages 15 miles per gallon of gas is driven 135 miles. The gas tank is then filled to capacity by pumping in 12 gallons of gas.
    If the gas tank holds 18 gallons when full, the amount of gas in the tank at the beginning of the 135 mile trip must have been _____ gallons.

    A. 6   B. 9   C. 12   D. 15

14. Suppose that a car ran a total of 9,888 miles in a four-month period from September through December, inclusive. It used 234 gallons of gas in September, 203 gallons in October, 191 gallons in November, and 196 gallons in December.
    The AVERAGE number of miles it traveled per gallon of gasoline was

    A. 10   B. 11   C. 12   D. 12 1/2

15. A government agency has a policy of replacing 1/3 of its vehicles each year. Of the 20 vehicles the agency is requesting in the budget, 95% are replacements.
    If the request is granted, the TOTAL number of vehicles in the agency will be

    A. 19   B. 27   C. 58   D. 61

16. Car A averaged 21 miles to a gallon of gas. Car B averaged 18 miles to a gallon of gas. Each car used 14 gallons of gas.
    How many miles more did car A travel than car B?

    A. 42   B. 39   C. 28   D. 14

17. A garage has a gas tank with a capacity of 500 gallons. During the week, 210 gallons were used and 340 gallons were delivered at the end of the week to fill the tank. How many gallons of gas were in the tank at the beginning of the week?

    A. 160   B. 210   C. 340   D. 370

18. The list price of vehicle A is $4,200 and that of vehicle B is $3,800. The city can get a discount of 20% of the list price on vehicle A and 10% of the list price on vehicle B. How much cheaper can the city buy vehicle A than vehicle B?

    A. $20   B. $60   C. $200   D. $600

19. In a certain bureau, there are 4 employees who each earn $250 a week, 12 employees who each earn $300 a week, and 2 employees who each earn $350 a week. The weekly payroll for all these employees is

    A. $4,900   B. $5,100   C. $5,300   D. $5,500

20. If the average passenger car needs 120 square feet of parking space, the LARGEST number of such cars that could be parked in a garage with a usable floor area that measures 70 feet by 100 feet is

    A. 52   B. 54   C. 56   D. 58

21. On a certain bridge, the toll for a motorcycle is 5/7 the toll for a passenger car and 1/3 the toll for a truck. If the toll for a passenger car is $1.75 then the toll for a truck on this bridge is

    A. $2.50   B. $3.75   C. $5.00   D. $6.25

22. If a car is traveling on a highway at a steady speed of 35 miles an hour, how many miles will it go in a period of 24 minutes?

    A. 13   B. 14   C. 15   D. 16

23. An employee's monthly salary is $7,625. If he receives a 5.4% salary increase, his new monthly salary will be

    A. $7,992.50   B. $8,036.75   C. $8,147.25   D. $8,169.00

24. Of the 60 drivers assigned to a garage, 1/6 of them live in County A, 1/4 of them live in County B, 1/5 of them live in County C, and the rest live in County D. How many of the drivers live in County D?

    A. 22   B. 23   C. 24   D. 25

25. Driver Green travels 33 miles along express highways at an average speed of 44 miles an hour to get to his destination. Driver Smith travels 28 miles through traffic at an average speed of 21 miles an hour to get to the same destination. If Mr. Smith starts his trip a half hour before Mr. Green, he will reach the destination _____ Mr. Green.

    A. 5 minutes before   B. at the same time as
    C. 5 minutes after   D. 10 minutes after

KEY (CORRECT ANSWERS)

1. D
2. A
3. B
4. D
5. A

6. D
7. A
8. A
9. C
10. A

11. D
12. C
13. D
14. C
15. C

16. A
17. D
18. B
19. C
20. D

21. B
22. B
23. B
24. B
25. C

SOLUTIONS TO PROBLEMS

1. 19,952 ÷ 14 1/2 = 1376 gallons of gas. Then, 1376 ÷ 21 1/2 = 64 quarts of oil

2. 26 ÷ .13 = 200 vehicles, including the trucks. The number of non-trucks = 200 - 26 = 174

3. [(4)($35,000)+(2)($31,500)+(1)($45,500)+(5)($38,000)] ÷ 12 = $36,541.67, closest to $36,500

4. (3 ft)(6 ft)(7 ft) = 126 cu.ft.

5. 520 ÷ 1300 = 40% full

6. [(1)(6)+(2)(12)+(2)(15)] ÷ 5 = 12 mos.

7. (162 1/2)(25 3/4) ÷ 84 ≈ 49.8, closest to 50 vehicles

8. 114 ÷ 44 = 28.5 . Then, (28.5)(23) ≈ 655 gallons

9. $45,800 - (.22)($45,800) - (.085)($45,800) - $1820 = $30,011
   Amount for every other week = $30,011 ÷ 26 ≈ $1154.20

10. ($12,500)(.80) - ($12,000)(.90) = -$800, so truck A is $800 cheaper than truck B.

11. Garage A holds (3/4)(88) =66 cars and garage C holds 66 ÷ 2/3 = 99 cars. Thus, all 3 garages hold 66 + 88 + 99 = 253 cars

12. Total cost = (5)($6000) + (3)($8000) + (2)($13,000) = $80,000

13. Let x = gallons of gas in the tank at the beginning.
    Then, x - 135/15 + 12 = 18. Solving, x = 15

14. Average = 9888 ÷ (234+203+191+196) = 12 miles per gallon

15. (20)(.95) = 19 replacements. Total number of vehicles = (19)(3) + 1 = 58

16. (21)(14) - (18)(14) = 42 miles

17. Let x = number of gallons in the tank at the beginning of the week. Then, x - 210 + 340 = 500. Solving, x = 370

18. ($3800)(.90) - ($4200)(.80) = $60. So, vehicle A is $60 cheaper than vehicle B.

19. (4)($250) + (12)($300) + (2)($350) = $5300

20. (70)(100) ÷ 120 = 58 .$\overline{3}$ so 58 cars is the maximum.

21. (5/7)($1.75) = $1.25 = toll for a motorcycle. Then, the toll for a truck = 1.25 ÷ 1/3 = $ 3.75

22. (35)(24/60) = 14 miles

23. ($7625)(1.054) = $8036.75

24. 60(1 - 1/6 - 1/4 - 1/5) = 23 drivers

25. Green requires 33/44 = 3/4hrs., whereas Smith requires 28/21 = 1 1/3 hr. Since Smith began 1/2 hr. sooner, he will reach his destination 1 1/3 - 1/2 - 3/4 = 1/12 = 5 min. after Green.

TEST 3

DIRECTIONS: Each question or incomplete statement is followed by several suggested answers or completions. Select the one that BEST answers the question or completes the statement. *PRINT THE LETTER OF THE CORRECT ANSWER IN THE SPACE AT THE RIGHT.*

1. Thirty miles per hour is equivalent to _____ feet per second. 1._____
   A. 30 B. 44 C. 60 D. 80

2. A driver whose car is parked for 8 hours in an off-street facility where the rate is 50 cents an hour for the first 5 hours and 75 cents an hour thereafter would pay 2._____
   A. $6.00 B. $5.75 C. $4.75 D. $4.00

3. An agent has written out 29 summonses for moving violations, 13 summonses for parking violations, and 3 summonses for other violations. 3._____
   The TOTAL number of summonses he has written out is
   A. 36 B. 42 C. 43 D. 45

4. A driver complains about being ticketed for parking too near a fire hydrant. He insists that his car is *at least 8 yards from the hydrant.* 4._____
   If he is right, how far away from the hydrant is his car, in terms of feet rather than yards?
   A. 16 B. 24 C. 30 D. 80

5. At the intersection of an avenue and a cross street, the traffic lights have been set so that traffic on the avenue has a green light for 55 seconds followed by a yellow light for 5 seconds, then traffic on the cross street has a green light for 25 seconds followed by a yellow light for 5 seconds. 5._____
   How long is a complete cycle of lights at this intersection, that is, how much time must pass from the moment the light turns from red to green until the moment the light will turn from red to green again?
   _____ seconds.
   A. 60 B. 70 C. 80 D. 90

6. An agent has jotted down the following notes on one day's work: 6._____
   8:00-11:30   On duty at intersection as assigned
   11:30 - 12:00 Off duty - lunch
   12:00-2:00   On duty - attending assigned training session
   2:00-4:00   On duty at intersection - replacement came late
   How many on-duty hours do this agent's notes show for this particular day?
   A. 4 B. 7 C. 7 1/2 D. 8

7. If a traffic jam of 78 vehicles occurs at the intersection you are controlling, and if one car can pass through the intersection every 10 seconds, how long will it take to clear these 78 vehicles out of the intersection? 7._____
   _____ minutes.
   A. 5.2 B. 7.8 C. 13.0 D. 15.7

8. An agent issued the following summonses in one day: 12 summonses at $25 each, 5 summonses at $15 each, and 3 summonses at $10 each.
What is the TOTAL amount of the fines for the summonses he gave out on that day?

   A. $305   B. $315   C. $405   D. $485

9. If the difference in elevation between two intersections 300 feet apart is 6 feet, the grade along the street is

   A. 2%   B. 2   C. 0.002   D. 6%

10. If on a highway a car passes a given point every 5 seconds, the number of cars per hour passing the given point on the highway is

    A. 360   B. 480   C. 600   D. 720

11. The cost of concrete paving for a strip of driveway 50 feet long, 10 feet wide, and 6 inches deep, if concrete in place costs $30 per cubic yard, is, in dollars, MOST NEARLY
(27 cubic feet = 1 cubic yard)

    A. 278   B. 318   C. 329   D. 380

12. The sketch at the right shows a right triangular island at the intersection of three streets on which is installed traffic signals A and B. Traffic conditions have increased and require that an additional traffic light be installed at point C. Electric power for signal C is to be taken from the junction box located at the base of post A and extended to C, as shown by the broken line.
With the distances given as shown, the length of conduit, in feet, required to extend power from A to C is MOST NEARLY

    A. 44   B. 60   C. 83   D. 75

13. The volume of traffic at a certain location increased from 1,000 to 1,500 vehicles per hour.
The percentage increase of traffic is MOST NEARLY

    A. 33%   B. 50%   C. 60%   D. 40%

14. During a certain three-month period, the bureau of enforcement issued 239,788 summonses. Of these, 37,900 were issued between the hours of 12 Noon and 1 P.M.; 33,350 were issued between 1 P.M. and 2 P.M.; and 23,334 were issued between 2 P.M. and 3 P.M.
What percentage of the total number of summonses issued during this three-month period was issued between 1 P.M. and 3 P.M.?

    A. 22%   B. 24%   C. 26%   D. 28%

15. A city has 51,489 parking meters. Thirteen percent of them require repairs.
Therefore, the number of meters requiring repairs is MOST NEARLY

    A. 6,690   B. 6,695   C. 6,700   D. 6,705

16. The following sums of money were collected from parking meters in an eight-week period: $15,298, $14,248, $16,873, $18,137, $18,256, $19,342, $18,437, and $15,432. Therefore, the total amount collected from these meters for this eight-week period was MOST NEARLY

    A. $135,150   B. $135,985   C. $136,025   D. $136,543

16._____

17. There were 68,937 meters in operation at the end of December. Exactly one year later, there were 102,331 meters in operation.
    Therefore, the increase in the number of meters in operation is MOST NEARLY

    A. 34,400   B. 33,900   C. 33,400   D. 32,900

17._____

18. In a certain city, there are 24,482 parking meters. Of these meters, 3/8 are in Zone A.
    Therefore, the number of meters in Zone A is MOST NEARLY

    A. 3,060   B. 8,160   C. 9,180   D. 12,240

18._____

19. It costs $55,525 to service 9,995 parking meters.
    Therefore, the cost of servicing one meter is MOST NEARLY

    A. $2.50   B. $3.50   C. $4.50   D. $5.50

19._____

20. Of 165 parking meters, 0.14 of the total are out of order.
    Therefore, the number of these parking meters out of order is MOST NEARLY

    A. 83   B. 23   C. 8   D. 2.31

20._____

21. Suppose that a city block on a parking meter collector's route is 260 feet wide by 780 feet long.
    Therefore, the area of this block, in square feet, is MOST NEARLY

    A. 1,040   B. 2,080   C. 104,000   D. 203,000

21._____

22. The base of a container for coin boxes measures 2 feet by 3 feet. The base of the coin boxes measures 2 inches by 3 inches.
    The GREATEST number of coin boxes that will fit into the container in a single layer is

    A. 36   B. 72   C. 100   D. 144

22._____

23. The total collected from parking meters in city A for a 12-month period was $701,790.
    Therefore, the average collected per month for this 12-month period was MOST NEARLY

    A. $58,481   B. $58,483   C. $58,485   D. $8,421,480

23._____

24. It costs $158.46 each week to maintain the parking meters in a certain city.
    Therefore, to maintain these meters for 372 weeks would cost MOST NEARLY

    A. $58,950   B. $58,975   C. $59,000   D. $59,025

24._____

25. Two attendants earn $6,240 and $6,220 per annum, respectively, exclusive of a bonus of $2,640 per annum.
    If both have a pension deduction of 20%, the difference in the pension deduction of the two attendants on a semimonthly basis is

    A. $1.50   B. $.50   C. $1.00   D. $.17

25._____

4 (#3)

KEY (CORRECT ANSWERS)

1. B
2. C
3. D
4. B
5. D

6. C
7. C
8. C
9. A
10. D

11. A
12. B
13. B
14. B
15. B

16. C
17. C
18. C
19. D
20. B

21. D
22. D
23. B
24. A
25. D

SOLUTIONS TO PROBLEMS

1. Since 60 mi/hr = 88 ft/sec, 30 mi/hr = 44 ft/sec
2. ($.50)(5) + ($.75)(3) = $4.75
3. 29 + 13 + 3 = 45 summonses
4. (8)(3) = 24 feet
5. One cycle = 55 + 5 + 25 + 5 = 90 seconds
6. 3 1/2 + 2 + 2 = 7 1/2 hrs. on duty
7. (78)(10) = 780 sec. = 13 min.
8. (12)($25) + (5)($15) + (3)($10) = $405
9. $\frac{6}{300}$ = .02 = 2% grade
10. 60 ÷ 5 = 12 per min. Then, (12)(60) = 720 cars per hr.
11. ($30)(50)(10)(1/2) ÷ 27 ≈ $278
12. Distance from A to C = $\sqrt{30^2 + 53^2} = \sqrt{3709} \approx 60$ ft.
13. $\frac{500}{1000}$ = 50% increase
14. (33,350+23,334) ÷ 239,788 = 56,684 ÷ 239,788 ≈ 24%
15. (51,489)(.13) = 6693.57, closest to 6695
16. $15,298 + $14,248 + $16,873 + $18,137 + $18,256 + $19,342 + $18,437 + $15,432 = $136,023, closest to $136,025
17. 102,331 - 68,937 = 33,394, closest to 33,400
18. (3/8)(24,482) = 9180.75, nearest to 9180
19. $55,525 ÷ 9995 ≈ $5.56, closest to $5.50
20. (.14)(165) = 23.1 ≈ 23
21. (260)(780) = 202,800 sq.ft. ≈ 203,000 sq.ft.
22. [(2')(3')] ÷ [(2/12')(3/12')] = 144 coin boxes maximum
23. $701,790 ÷ 12 = $58,483
24. ($158.46)(372) = $58,947.12 ≈ $58,950
25. ($6240-$6220)(.20) = $4 per year. This equates to $4 ÷ 24 ≈ 17 cents per half-month.

HIGHWAY TRAFFIC SIGNALS

CONTENTS

	Page
A. General	
Section A-1. Types	1
A-2. Basis of Installation	1
B. Traffic Control Signals	
Section B-1. General Aspects	1
B-2. Area of Control	1
B-3. Advantages and Disadvantages of Traffic Control Signals	2
B-4. Portable Traffic Control Signals	2
B-5. Meaning of Signal Indications	2
B-6. Application of Signal Indications	4
B-7. Number of Lenses per Signal Face	6
B-8. Size and Design of Signal Lenses	6
B-9. Arrangement of Lenses in Signal Faces	7
B-10. Illumination of Lenses	9
B-11. Visibility and Shielding of Signal Faces	10
B-12. Number and Locations of Signal Faces	10
B-13. Height of Signal Faces	13
B-14. Transverse Location of Traffic Signal Supports and Controller Cabinets	13
B-15. Vehicle Change Interval	14
B-16. Unexpected Conflicts During Green Interval	14
B-17. Coordination of Traffic Control Signals	15
B-18. Flashing Operation of Traffic Control Signals	15
B-19. Continuity of Operation	16
B-20. Signal Operation Must Relate to Traffic Flow	16
B-21. Traffic Signals Near Grade Crossings	16
B-22. Emergency Operation of Traffic Signals	17
B-23. Maintenance of Traffic Control Signals	18
B-24. Painting	19
B-25. Vehicle Detectors	19
B-26. Auxiliary Signs	19
B-27. Removal of Confusing Advertising Lights	20

HIGHWAY TRAFFIC SIGNALS

A. GENERAL

A-1 Types

This part relates to a group of devices called highway traffic signals. These devices include: traffic control signals, beacons, lane-use control signals, drawbridge signals, emergency traffic control signals and train approach signals and gates. Only the first of these will be discussed in this section.

A-2 Basis of Installation

In most cases the installation of a highway traffic control signal will operate either to the advantage or disadvantage of the vehicles and persons controlled. A careful analysis of traffic operations and other factors at a large number of signalized and unsignalized intersections, coupled with the judgment of experienced engineers, have provided a series of warrants that define the minimum conditions under which signal installations may be justified. Consequently the selection and use of this control device should be preceded by a thorough engineering study of roadway and traffic conditions.

Engineering studies should be made of operating signals to determine if the type of installation and the timing program meet the current requirements of traffic.

B. TRAFFIC CONTROL SIGNALS

B-1 General Aspects

There are two types of traffic control signals, pretimed and traffic-actuated.

The features of traffic control signals in which vehicle operators and pedestrians are interested are the location, design, indications, and legal significance of the signals. These are identical for all types of traffic control signals. Uniformity in the design features that affect the traffic to be controlled (as set forth in this Manual) is especially important for safe and efficient traffic operations.

Special police supervision and/or enforcement should be provided for a new non-intersection location.

B-2 Area of Control

A traffic control signal shall control traffic only at the intersection or mid-block location where the installation is placed.

B-3 Advantages and Disadvantages of Traffic Control Signals

Traffic control signals are valuable devices for the control of vehicle and pedestrian traffic. However, because they assign the right-of-way to the various traffic movements, traffic control signals exert a profound influence on traffic flow.

Traffic control signals, properly located and operated usually have one or more of the following advantages:

1. They can provide for the orderly movement of traffic.
2. Where proper physical layouts and control measures are used, they can increase the traffic-handling capacity of the intersection.
3. They can reduce the frequency of certain types of accidents, especially the right-angle type.
4. Under favorable conditions, they can be coordinated to provide for continuous or nearly continuous movement of traffic at a definite speed along a given route.
5. They can be used to interrupt heavy traffic at intervals to permit other traffic, vehicular or pedestrian, to cross.

Many laymen believe that traffic signals provide the solution to all traffic problems at intersections. This has led to their installation at a large number of locations where no legitimate factual warrant exists.

Traffic signal installations, even though warranted by traffic and roadway conditions, can be ill-designed, ineffectively placed, improperly operated, or poorly maintained. The following factors can result from improper or unwarranted signal installations:

1. Excessive delay may be caused.
2. Disobedience of the signal indications is encouraged.
3. The use of less adequate routes may be induced in an attempt to avoid such signals.
4. Accident frequency (especially the rear-end type) can be significantly increased.

B-4 Portable Traffic Control Signals

A portable traffic control signal not meeting all the requirements is not recognized as a standard traffic control device.

B-5 Meaning of Signal Indications

The following meanings shall be given to highway traffic signal indications, except those on pedestrian signals:

1. Green indications shall have the following meanings:
  a. Traffic, except pedestrians, facing a CIRCULAR GREEN may proceed straight through or turn right or left unless a sign at such place prohibits either such turn. But vehicular traffic, includ-

ing vehicles turning right or left, shall yield the right-of-way to other vehicles, and to pedestrians lawfully within the intersection or an adjacent crosswalk, at the time such signal is exhibited.

b. Traffic, except pedestrians, facing a GREEN ARROW, shown alone or in combination with another indication, may cautiously enter the intersection only to make the movement indicated by such arrow, or such other movement as is permitted by other indications shown at the same time. Such vehicular traffic shall yield the right-of-way to pedestrians lawfully within an adjacent crosswalk and to other traffic lawfully using the intersection.

c. Unless otherwise directed by a pedestrian signal, pedestrians facing any green indication, except when the sole green indication is a turn arrow, may proceed across the roadway within any marked or unmarked crosswalk.

2. Steady yellow indications shall have the following meanings:

a. Traffic, except pedestrians, facing a steady CIRCULAR YELLOW or YELLOW ARROW signal is thereby warned that the related green movement is being terminated or that a red indication will be exhibited immediately thereafter when vehicular traffic shall not enter the intersection.

b. Pedestrians facing a steady CIRCULAR YELLOW or YELLOW ARROW signal, unless otherwise directed by a pedestrian signal, are thereby advised that there is insufficient time to cross the roadway before a red indication is shown and no pedestrian shall then start to cross the roadway.

3. Steady red indications shall have the following meanings:

a. Traffic, except pedestrians, facing a steady CIRCULAR RED signal alone shall stop at a clearly marked stop line, but if none, before entering the crosswalk on the near side of the intersection, or if none, then before entering the intersection and shall remain standing until an indication to proceed is shown except as provided in b below.

b. When a sign is in place permitting a turn, traffic, except pedestrians, facing a steady CIRCULAR RED signal may cautiously enter the intersection to make the turn indicated by such sign after stopping as provided in a above. Such vehicular traffic shall yield the right-of-way to pedestrians lawfully within an adjacent crosswalk and to other traffic lawfully using the intersection.

c. Unless otherwise directed by a pedestrian signal, pedestrians facing a steady CIRCULAR RED signal alone shall not enter the roadway.

d. Traffic, except pedestrians, facing a steady RED ARROW indication may not enter the intersection to make the movement indicated by such arrow, and unless entering the intersection to make such other movement as is permitted by other indications shown at the same time, shall stop at a clearly marked stop line, but if none, before entering the crosswalk on the near side of the intersection, or if none, then before entering the intersection and shall remain standing until an indication to make the movement indicated by such arrow is shown.

e. Unless otherwise directed by a pedestrian signal, pedestrians facing a steady RED ARROW signal indication shall not enter the roadway.

4. Flashing signal indications shall have the following meanings:

a. Flashing red (stop signal)—When a red lens is illuminated with rapid intermittent flashes, drivers of vehicles shall stop at a clearly marked stop line, but if none, before entering the crosswalk on the near side of the intersection, or if none, then at the point nearest the intersecting roadway where the driver has a view of approaching traffic on the intersecting roadway before entering the intersection, and the right to proceed shall be subject to the rules applicable after making a stop at a STOP sign.

b. Flashing yellow (caution signal)—When a yellow lens is illuminated with rapid intermittent flashes, drivers of vehicles may proceed through the intersection or past such signal only with caution.

B-6 Application of Signal Indications

Basic displays used in signal operations are the steady CIRCULAR RED, CIRCULAR YELLOW or CIRCULAR GREEN indication, used on each of the approaches. The application for these signal indications shall be as follows:

1. A steady CIRCULAR RED indication:

a. Shall be given when it is intended to prohibit traffic from entering the intersection or other controlled area.

b. Should be displayed with the appropriate green arrow indications when it is intended to permit traffic to make a specified turn or turns, and to prohibit traffic from proceeding straight ahead through the controlled area. This display is optional where it is physically impossible for traffic to go straight ahead, as at the head of a "T" intersection.

c. Shall be given when it is intended to prohibit all traffic, except pedestrians directed by a pedestrian signal, from entering the intersection or other controlled area.

2. A steady CIRCULAR YELLOW indication:

a. Shall be given following a CIRCULAR GREEN indication in the same signal face.

b. Is an optional alternative to a yellow arrow indication following a green arrow indication in a separate signal face used exclusively to control a single directional movement.

3. A steady CIRCULAR GREEN indication shall be given only when it is intended to permit traffic to proceed in any direction which is lawful and practical.

4. Steady RED ARROW, YELLOW ARROW and GREEN ARROW indications may be used in lieu of the corresponding circular indications at the following locations:

a. On an approach intersecting a one-way street.

b. Where certain movements are prohibited.

c. Where certain movements are physically impossible.

d. On an intersection approach which has an exclusive lane for turning movements.

e. Where turning movements are "protected" from conflicting movements by other indications or by the signal sequence.

f. Where all the movements on the approach do not begin or end at the same time and where the indications for the turning movements will also be visible to traffic with other allowable movements.

If steady arrow indications are used:

a. A steady RED ARROW indication shall be used only in a separate signal face which also contains steady YELLOW ARROW and GREEN ARROW indications. It shall be used for controlling only a single traffic movement.

b. A steady YELLOW ARROW indication shall be used following a GREEN ARROW indication (which has been displayed simultaneously with a CIRCULAR RED indication in the same signal face).

c. A steady YELLOW ARROW indication may be used (in a separate signal face) following a GREEN ARROW indication, when that face is used exclusively to control a single directional movement.

d. A steady YELLOW ARROW indication may be used to indicate the clearance interval following the termination of a GREEN ARROW indication (when displayed simultaneously with a continuing CIRCULAR GREEN indication in the same signal face).

e. A steady GREEN ARROW indication shall be used only when there would be no conflict with other vehicles or with pedestrians crossing in conformance with the WALK indication.

5. The following combinations of signal indications shall not be simultaneously displayed on any one signal face, and shall not be simultaneously displayed in different signal faces on any one approach to an intersection unless the signal faces are shielded, hooded, louvered, positioned or designed so that none of these prohibited combinations of signal indications is readily visible to drivers:

    a. CIRCULAR GREEN with CIRCULAR YELLOW.

    b. Straight-through GREEN ARROW with CIRCULAR RED.

    c. CIRCULAR RED with CIRCULAR YELLOW.

    d. CIRCULAR GREEN with CIRCULAR RED.

    e. CIRCULAR GREEN with RED ARROW.

6. When a traffic control signal is put on flashing operation, normally a yellow indication should be used for the major street and a red indication for the other approaches. Yellow indications shall not be used for all approaches. The following applications shall apply whenever signals are placed in flashing operation:

    a. A CIRCULAR YELLOW indication shall be flashed instead of any YELLOW ARROW indication which may be included in that signal face.

    b. No CIRCULAR GREEN or GREEN ARROW indication or flashing yellow indication shall be terminated and immediately followed by a steady red or flashing red indication without the display of the steady yellow change indication; however, transition may be made directly from a CIRCULAR GREEN or GREEN ARROW indication to a flashing yellow indication.

B-7 Number of Lenses per Signal Face

Each signal face, except in pedestrian signals, shall have at least three lenses, but not more than five. The lenses shall be red, yellow or green in color, and shall give a circular or arrow type of indication. Allowable exceptions to the above are:

1. Where a single section green arrow lens is used alone to indicate a continuous movement.

2. As discussed under Unexpected Conflicts During Green Interval (sec. B-16).

3. Where one or more indications are repeated for reasons of safety or impact.

B-8 Size and Design of Signal Lenses

The aspect of all signal lenses, except in pedestrian signals, shall be circular. There shall be two sizes for lenses, 8 inches and 12 inches nominal diameter.

Twelve-inch lenses normally should be used:

1. For intersections with 85 percentile approach speeds exceeding 40 mph.

2. For intersections where signalization might be unexpected.

3. For special problem locations, such as those with conflicting or competing background lighting.

4. For intersections where drivers may view both traffic control and lane-direction-control signs simultaneously.

5. For all arrow indications.

Arrows shall be pointed vertically upward to indicate a straight-through movement and in a horizontal direction to indicate a turn at approximately right angles. When the angle of the turn is substantially different from a right angle, the arrow should be positioned on an upward slope at an angle approximately equal to that of the turn.

Each arrow lens shall show only one arrow direction. The arrow shall be the only illuminated part of the lens visible.

In no case shall letters or numbers be displayed as part of a vehicular signal indication.

Except for the requirements of this section, all lenses shall conform to the Standard for Adjustable Face Vehicle Traffic Control Signal Heads, 1970 Edition.

B-9 Arrangement of Lenses in Signal Faces

The lenses in a signal face shall be arranged in a vertical or horizontal straight line, except that in a vertical array, lenses of the same color may be arranged horizontally adjacent to each other at right angles to the basic straight line arrangement (fig. 4-1). Such clusters shall be limited to two identical lenses or to two or three different lenses of the same color.

In each signal face, all red lenses in vertical signals shall be located above, and in horizontal signals shall be located to the left of all yellow and green lenses.

A CIRCULAR YELLOW lens shall be located between the red lens or lenses and all other lenses.

In vertically arranged signal faces, each YELLOW ARROW lens shall be located immediately above the GREEN ARROW lens to which it applies. In horizontally arranged signals, the YELLOW ARROW shall be located immediately to the left of the GREEN ARROW lens.

8

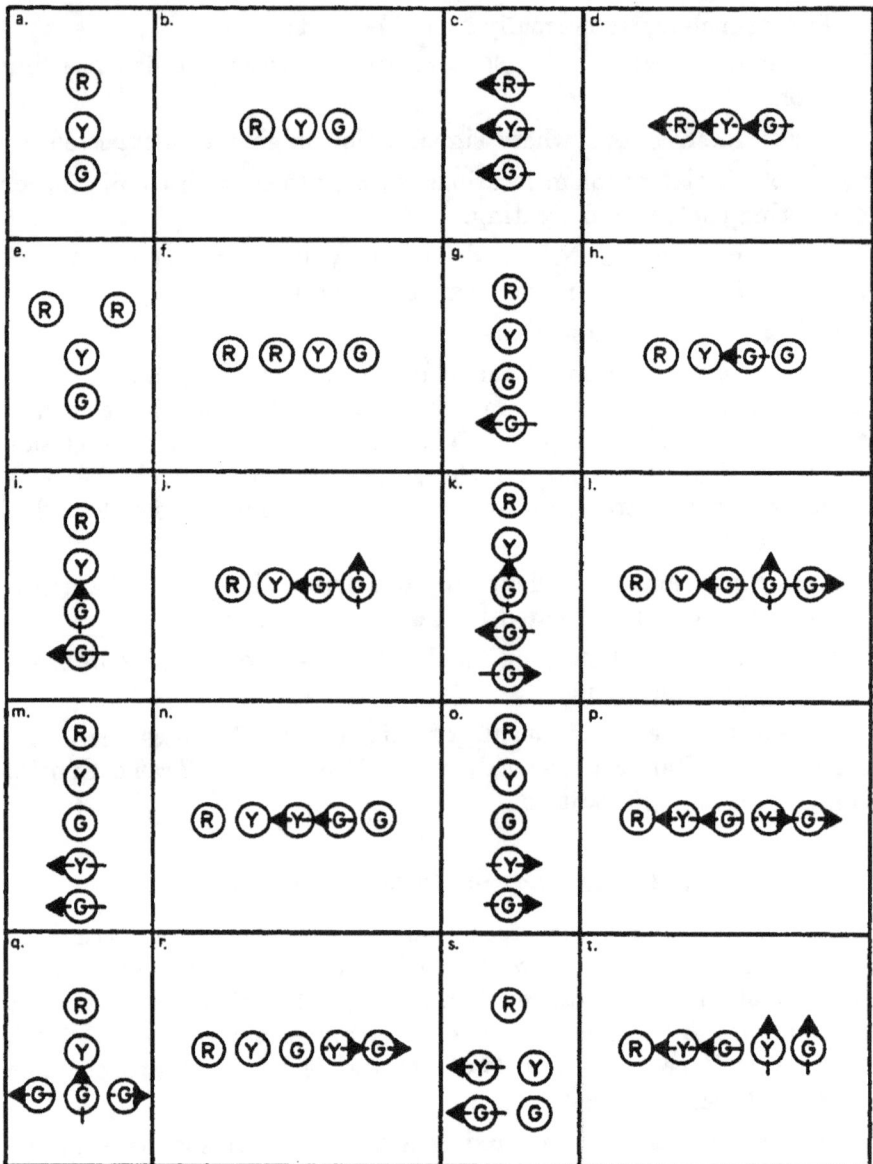

Figure 1. Typical arrangements of lenses in signal faces.

The relative positions of lenses within the signal face shall be as follows:

1. In a vertical signal face from top to bottom:
    CIRCULAR RED
    Left turn RED ARROW
    Right turn RED ARROW
    CIRCULAR YELLOW

Straight through YELLOW ARROW
Straight through GREEN ARROW
CIRCULAR GREEN
Left turn YELLOW ARROW
Left turn GREEN ARROW
Right turn YELLOW ARROW
Right turn GREEN ARROW

2. In a horizontal signal face from left to right:
CIRCULAR RED
Left turn RED ARROW
Right turn RED ARROW
CIRCULAR YELLOW
Left turn YELLOW ARROW
Left turn GREEN ARROW
CIRCULAR GREEN
Straight through YELLOW ARROW
Straight through GREEN ARROW
Right turn YELLOW ARROW
Right turn GREEN ARROW

3. In a cluster, identical signal indications may be repeated in adjacent vertical or horizontal locations within the same signal face. If adjacent indications in a cluster are not identical, their arrangement shall follow paragraph 1 or 2 above, as applicable.

Basic horizontal and vertical display faces may be used on the same approach provided they are separated to meet the lateral clearance required in section B-12.

Figure 1 shows some possible arrangements of lenses in signal faces.

B-10 Illumination of Lenses

Each signal lens shall be illuminated independently.

When a signal lens, except in a pedestrian signal, is illuminated and the view of such an indication is not otherwise physically obstructed, it shall be clearly visible (to drivers it controls) for a distance of a least ¼ mile under normal atmospheric conditions.

The intensity and distribution of light from each illuminated signal lens should conform to the Standard for Adjustable Face Vehicle Traffic Control Signal Heads, Revised 1970; and the Standard for Traffic Signal Lamps, December 1967.

When 12" lens signals with 150 watt lamps are placed on flashing for nighttime operation and the flashing yellow indication is so bright as to cause excessive glare, an automatic dimming device should be used to reduce the brilliance of the flashing 12" yellow.

B-11 Visibility and Shielding of Signal Faces

Each signal face shall be so adjusted that its indications will be of maximum effectiveness to the approaching traffic for which they are intended.

Visors should be used on all signal faces to aid in directing the signal indication specifically to approaching traffic, as well as to reduce "sun phantom" resulting from external light entering the lens. Back-plates normally should be used on one-way and back-to-back two-way overhead signals, and when one signal face controls a movement.

In general, vehicular signal faces should be aimed to have maximum effectiveness for an approaching driver located a distance from the stop line equal to the distance traversed while stopping. This distance should include that covered while reacting to the signal as well as that covered while bringing the vehicle to a stop from an average approach speed. The influence of curves, grades, and obstructions should be considered in directing and locating signals.

Irregular street design frequently necessitates placing signals for different street approaches with a comparatively small angle between their indications. In these cases, each signal indication shall, to the extent practicable, be shielded or directed by visors, louvers, or other means so that an approaching driver can see only the indication controlling his movement. Tunnel visors exceeding 12" in length shall not be used on free-swinging signals.

The foregoing does not preclude the use of special signal faces such that the driver does not see their indications before seeing other indications further ahead, when simultaneous viewing of both signal indications could cause the driver to be misdirected.

B-12 Number and Location of Signal Faces

The primary consideration in signal face placement shall be visibility. Drivers approaching a signalized intersection or other signalized area, such as a mid-block crosswalk, shall be given a clear and unmistakable indication of their right-of-way assignment. Critical elements are lateral and vertical angles of sight toward a signal face, as determined by typical driver eye position, vehicle design, and the vertical, longitudinal and lateral position of the signal face. The geometry of each intersection to be signalized, including vertical grades and horizontal curves, should be considered in signal face placement.

The visibility, location and number of signal faces for each approach to an intersection or a mid-block crosswalk shall be as follows:

1. A minimum of two signal faces for through-traffic shall be provided and should be continuously visible from a point at least the following distances in advance of and to the stop line, unless physical obstruction of their visibility exists:

85 Percentile Speed	Minimum Visibility Distance (Ft.)
20	100
25	175
30	250
35	325
40	400
45	475
50	550
55	625
60	700

2. Where physical conditions prevent drivers from having a continuous view of at least two signal indications as specified herein, a suitable sign shall be erected to warn approaching traffic. It may be supplemented by a Hazard Identification Beacon.
A beacon utilized in this manner may be interconnected with the traffic signal controller in such a manner as to flash yellow during the period when drivers passing this beacon, at the legal speed for the roadway, may encounter a red signal upon arrival at the signalized location.

3. A single signal face is permissible for the control of an exclusive turn lane. Such a signal face shall be in addition to the minimum of two signal faces for through-traffic. When the indications of a separate signal face or faces controlling an exclusive turn lane will also be visible to traffic with other allowable movements, a sign LEFT (or RIGHT) TURN SIGNAL shall be located adjacent to such signal face. When the face consists entirely of arrow indications, such a sign is not required.

4. Except where the width of the intersecting street or other conditions make it physically impractical, at least one and preferably both of the signal faces required by paragraph (1) above shall be located not less than 40 feet nor more than 120 feet beyond the stop line. Where both of the signal faces required by paragraph (1) above are post-mounted, they shall both be on the far side of the intersection, one on the right and one on the left or on the median island if practical. The signal face required by paragraph (3) above shall conform to the same location requirements as the signal faces required by paragraph (1) to the extent practical.

5. Except where the width of the intersecting street or other conditions make it physically impractical, at least one and preferably

both of the signal faces required by paragraph (1) above shall be located between two lines intersecting with the center of the approach lanes at the stop line, one making an angle of approximately 20 degrees to the right of the center of the approach extended, and the other making an angle of approximately 20 degrees to the left of the center of the approach extended (fig. 2).

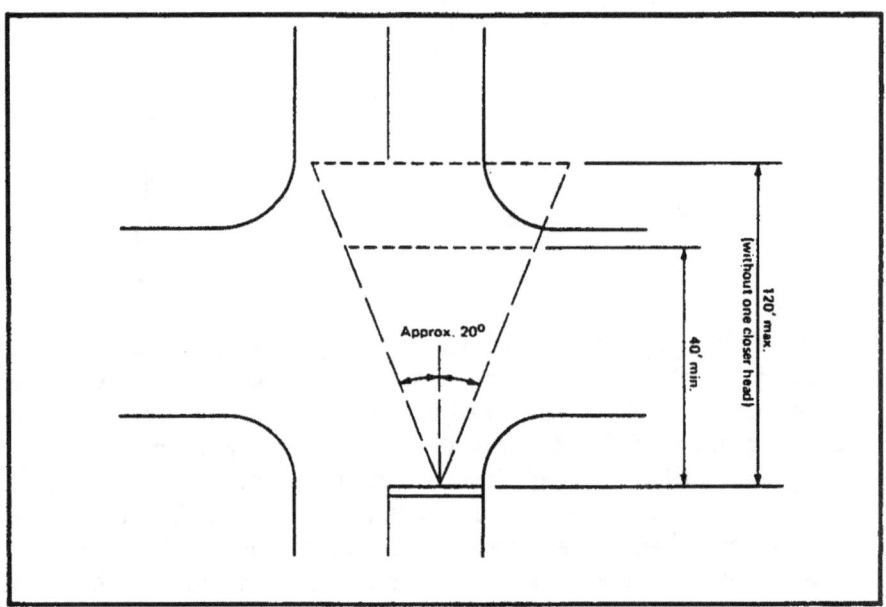

Figure 2. Desirable location of signal faces.

6. Near-side signals should be located as near as practicable to the stop line.

7. Where a signal face controls a specific lane or lanes of approach, its transverse position should be unmistakably in line with the path of that movement.

8. Required signal faces for any one approach shall be not less than eight feet apart measured horizontally between centers of faces.

9. When the nearest signal face is more than 120 feet beyond the stop line, a supplemental near side signal indication shall be provided.

10. A signal face mounted on a span wire or mast arm should be located as near as practicable to the line of the driver's normal view.

11. Supplemental signal faces should be used when an engineering study has shown that they are needed to achieve both advance and immediate intersection visibility. When used, they should be lo-

cated to provide optimum visibility for the movement to be controlled. The following limitations apply:

 a. Left turn arrows shall not be used in near-right faces.

 b. Right turn arrows shall not be used in far-left faces. A farside median mount signal shall be considered as a far-left signal for this application.

At signalized mid-block crosswalks, there should be at least one signal face over the traveled roadway for each approach. In other respects, a traffic control signal at a mid-block location shall meet the requirements set forth herein.

The transverse location of a signal face, shall, if mounted on the top of a post or on a short bracket from it, conform with section B-14.

Supplementary pedestrian signals shall be used where warranted.

B-13 Height of Signal Faces

The bottom of the housing of a signal face, not mounted over a roadway, shall not be less than 8 feet nor more than 15 feet above the sidewalk or, if none, above the pavement grade at the center of the highway.

The bottom of the housing of a signal face suspended over a roadway shall not be less than 15 feet nor more than 19 feet above the pavement grade at the center of the roadway.

Within the above limits, optimum visibility and adequate clearance should be the guiding considerations in deciding signal height. Grades on approaching streets may be important factors, and should be considered in determining the most appropriate height.

B-14 Transverse Location of Traffic Signal Supports and Controller Cabinets

In the placement of signal supports, primary consideration shall be given to ensuring the proper visibility of signal faces as described in sections B-12 and 13. However, in the interest of safety, signal supports and controller cabinets should be placed as far as practicable from the edge of the traveled way without adversely affecting signal visibility.

Supports for post-mounted signal heads at the side of a street with curbs shall have a horizontal clearance of not less than two feet from the face of a vertical curb. Where there is no curb, supports for post-mounted signal heads shall have a horizontal clearance of not less than two feet from the edge of a shoulder, within the limits of normal vertical clearance. A signal support should not obstruct a crosswalk.

No part of a concrete base for a signal support should extend more than 4 inches above the ground level at any point, except that this limitation does not apply to the concrete base for a rigid (non-breakaway) support.

On medians, the above minimum clearances for signal supports should be obtained where practicable. Any supports which cannot be located with the required clearances should be of the breakaway type or should be guarded if at all practicable.

B-15 Vehicle Change Interval

A yellow vehicle change interval shall be used following each CIRCULAR GREEN interval and, where applicable after each GREEN ARROW interval. In no case shall a CIRCULAR YELLOW indication be displayed in conjunction with the change from CIRCULAR RED to CIRCULAR GREEN. Separate signal faces should be used when exclusive turning movements are controlled by GREEN ARROWS (sec. B-6).

The exclusive function of the steady yellow interval shall be to warn traffic of an impending change in the right-of-way assignment.

Yellow vehicle change intervals should have a range of approximately 3 to 6 seconds. Generally the longer intervals are appropriate to higher approach speeds.

The yellow vehicle change interval may be followed by a short all-way red clearance interval, of sufficient duration to permit the intersection to clear before cross traffic is released.

A clearance interval shall be provided between the termination of a GREEN ARROW indication and the showing of a green indication to any conflicting traffic movement.

B-16 Unexpected Conflicts During Green Interval

No movement that may involve an unexpected crossing of pathways of moving traffic should be indicated during any green interval, except when:

1. The movement involves only slight hazard;
2. Serious traffic delays are materially reduced by permitting the conflicting movement; and
3. Drivers and pedestrians subjected to the unexpected conflict are effectively warned thereof.

When such conditions of possible unexpected conflict exist, warning may be given by a sign or, by the use of an appropriate signal indication as set forth in section B-7. The foregoing applies to vehicle-pedestrian conflicts as well as to vehicle-vehicle conflicts.

B-17 Coordination of Traffic Control Signals

Traffic control signals within one-half of a mile of one another along a major route or in a network of intersecting major routes should be operated in coordination, preferably with interconnected controllers. However, coordination need not be maintained across boundaries between signal systems which operate on different time cycles. Coordinated operation normally should include both pretimed signals and traffic-actuated signals within the appropriate distances.

For coordination with railroad grade crossings signals see section B-21.

B-18 Flashing Operation of Traffic Control Signals

All traffic signal installations shall be provided with an electrical flashing mechanism supplementary to the signal timer. A manual switch, or where appropriate, automatic means, shall be provided to actuate the flashing mechanism. The signal timer shall be removable without affecting the flashing operation. The mechanism shall operate in a manner similar to that of an Intersection Control Beacon to provide intermittent illumination of selected signal lenses.

The illuminating element in a flashing signal shall be flashed continuously at a rate of not less than 50 nor more than 60 times per minute. The illuminated period of each flash shall be not less than half and not more than two-thirds of the total flash cycle.

When traffic control signals are put on flashing operation, the signal indications given to the several streets shall be as specified in section B-6.

Automatic changes from flashing to stop-and-go operation shall be made at the beginning of the major street green interval, preferably at the beginning of the common major street green interval, (i.e., when a green indication is shown in both directions on the major street). Automatic changes from stop-and-go to flashing operation shall be made at the end of the common major street red interval, (i.e., when a red indication is shown in both directions on the major street).

The change from the flashing to stop-and-go operation, or from stop-and-go to flashing operation by manual switch may be made at any time.

Where there is no common major street green interval, the automatic change from flashing to stop-and-go operation shall be made at the beginning of the green interval for the major traffic movement on the major street. It may be necessary to provide a short, steady all-red interval for the other approaches before changing from flashing yellow or flashing red to green on the major approach.

B-19 Continuity of Operation

A traffic signal installation, except as provided below, shall be operated as a stop-and-go device or as a flashing device.

When a signal installation is not in operation such as prior to placing it in service, during seasonal shutdowns, or when it is not desirable to operate the signals, they should be hooded, turned or taken down to clearly indicate that the signal is not in operation.

When a traffic signal installation is being operated in the usual (stop-and-go) manner, at least one indication in each signal face shall be illuminated.

When a traffic signal installation is being operated as a flashing device, the yellow indication shall be flashed in at least two required signal faces (sec. B-12) on each approach on which traffic is not stopped and the red indication shall be flashed in at least two required signal faces (sec. B-12) on each approach on which traffic is required to stop.

The above provisions do not apply to emergency-traffic signals or draw-bridge signals.

When a single-section, continuously illuminated GREEN ARROW lens is used alone to indicate a continuous movement, it may be continuously illuminated when the other signal indications in the signal installation are flashed.

B-20 Signal Operation Must Relate to Traffic Flow

Traffic control signals shall be operated in a manner consistent with traffic requirements. Data from engineering studies shall be used to determine the proper phasing and timing for a signal.

Since traffic flows and patterns change, it is necessary that the engineering data be updated and re-evaluated regularly.

To assure that the approved operating pattern including timing is displayed to the driver, regular checks including the use of accurate timing devices should be made.

B-21 Traffic Signals Near Grade Crossings

When a railroad grade crossing, protected by train-approach signals is within or near an intersection controlled by a traffic control signal, the control of the traffic signal should be preempted from the signal controller upon approach of trains to avoid conflicting aspects of the traffic signal and the train-approach signal. This preemption feature requires a closed electrical circuit between the control relay of the train-approach signals and the preemptor in order to establish and maintain the preempted condition during the time that the train-approach signals are in operation. Except under unusual circumstances, the interconnection should be limited to the traffic signals within 200 feet of the crossing.

Traffic control signals shall not be used on mainline railroad crossings in lieu of railroad grade crossing protection devices. However, at industrial track crossings and other places where train movements are very slow (as in switching operations), traffic control signals may be used in lieu of conventional train-approach signals to warn motorists of the approach or presence of a train. The provisions of this part relating to traffic signal design, installation and operation are applicable as appropriate where traffic control signals are so used.

At crossings where train movements are regulated or limited to the extent that train-approach signals are not required, preemption of the adjacent signalized intersections may be desirable to permit non-conflicting highway traffic to proceed during the time the crossing is blocked by a train. Except under unusual circumstances, the interconnection should be limited to the traffic signals within 200 feet of the crossing.

The preemption sequence initiated when the train first enters the approach circuit, shall at once bring into effect a signal display which will permit all vehicles to clear the tracks before the train reaches the intersection or any approach thereto.

When the green indication is preempted by train operation, a yellow change interval must be inserted in the signal sequence in the interest of safety and consistency. To avoid misinterpretation during the time that the clear-out signals are green, consideration should be given to the use of 12-inch red lenses in the signals which govern movement over the tracks (sec. B-8).

After the track clearance phase, the traffic control signal may be operated to permit vehicle movements that do not cross the tracks, but in all cases shall prohibit movements over the tracks.

Where feasible the location and the normal (no trains involved) phasing and timing of traffic control signals near railroad grade crossings should be designed so that vehicles are not required to stop on the tracks even though in some cases this will increase the waiting time. The exact nature of the display and the location of the signals to accomplish this will depend on the physical relationship of the tracks to the intersection area.

When the train clears the crossing it is necessary to return the signal to a designated phase, normally the traffic movement crossing the tracks.

As used herein, the terms "train" and "railroad" shall include transit vehicles operating upon stationary rails or tracks on private right-of-way.

B-22 Emergency Operation of Traffic Signals

Systems in which traffic control signals are preempted by emergency vehicles shall operate to permit a normal change interval to take place in the change from green to yellow to red (or flashing red) before arrival of the emergency vehicle at the preempted location. Systems in which traffic control signals are preempted by emergency vehicles shall be designed and installed so as to provide an indication to the driver of any emergency vehicle approaching an intersection when the equipment fails to preempt the traffic signal at that intersection. This indication shall be designed to be given whether the failure results from a prior preemption by an emergency vehicle on the cross street, by a railroad preemption, from equipment malfunction, or from any other cause.

Traffic signals operating in congested areas during emergency conditions should be operated in a manner designed to keep traffic moving. Prolonged all-red or flashing signal sequences are to be avoided.

B-23 Maintenance of Traffic Control Signals

Prior to the installation of any traffic control signal, the responsibility for its maintenance should be clearly established. The responsible agency should provide for the maintenance of the signal and all of its appurtenances in a responsible manner. To this end the agency should:

1. Provide for alternate operation of the signal during a period of failure, either on flash or manually, or by having manual traffic direction by proper authority as may be warranted by traffic volumes or congestion, or by erecting other traffic control devices.

2. Have properly skilled maintenance available without undue delay for all emergency calls, including lamp failures.

3. Provide properly skilled maintenance for all components.

4. Maintain the appearance of the installation in a manner consistent with the intention of this part, with particular emphasis on painting and on cleaning of the optical system.

5. Service equipment and lamps as frequently as experience proves necessary to prevent undue failures.

6. Provide adequate stand-by equipment to minimize the interruption of signal operation due to equipment failure.

Every controller should be kept in effective operation in strict accordance with its predetermined timing schedule.

A careful check of the correctness of time operation of the controller should be made frequently enough to insure its operating in accordance with the planned timing schedule. Timing changes should be made only by authorized persons. A written record should be made of all timing changes.

Controllers should be carefully cleaned and serviced at least as frequently as specified by the manufacturer and more frequently if experience proves it necessary.

B-24 Painting

The insides of visors (hoods) and the entire surface of louvers, and fins, and the front surface of backplates shall have a dull black finish to minimize light reflection to the side of the signals.

To obtain the best possible contrast with the visual background, it is desirable to paint signal head housings highway yellow.

B-25 Vehicle Detectors

The placement of vehicle detectors in relation to the Stop line is a very important factor in the proper operation of traffic actuated signals and should be a factor in signal design.

Where the total entering traffic on one street is more than twice that on the cross street, detectors on the cross street should be placed closer to the stop line than on the main street.

Additional "calling" detectors may be required on lower volume streets to handle traffic entering the street from driveways between the basic detector and the Stop line.

The transverse placement of detectors should be such that vehicles traveling away from the intersection do not register "false-calls." On narrow two-way roadways this may require use of directional detectors.

B-26 Auxiliary Signs

Signal instruction signs used with traffic signals shall be located adjacent to the signal face to which they apply. Minimum clearance of the total assembly shall conform to the provisions of sections A-23 and B-13.

Stop signs shall not be used in conjunction with any signal operation, except:

1. When the indication flashes red at all times or
2. When a minor street or driveway is located within or adjacent to the controlled area, but does not warrant separate signal control due to extremely low potential for conflict.

When used in conjunction with traffic signals, illuminated signs shall be designed and mounted in such a manner as to avoid glare and reflections that seriously detract from the signal indications. The traffic control signal shall be given dominant position and brightness to assure its target priority in the overall display.

Traffic Signal Speed signs may be used to inform drivers of the speed of progression, if this speed is substantially lower than the speed limits in effect on streets in the signal system.

B-27 Removal of Confusing Advertising Lights

There should be legal authority to prohibit the display of any unauthorized sign, signal, marking, or device which interferes with the effectiveness of any official traffic control device. Specific reference is made to Section 11-205, Uniform Vehicle Code—Revised 1968.

GLOSSARY OF TRAFFIC CONTROL TERMS

TABLE OF CONTENTS

	Page
Access Road ... Desire Line	1
Divided Street ... Left Turn Lane	2
Manual Traffic Control ... Passenger Vehicle	3
Passenger (Transit) Volume ... Separate Turning Lane	4
Shoulder ... Traffic Accident	5
Traffic Actuated Controller ... Uninterrupted Flow	6
Vehicle ... Zone (Origin-Destination Studies)	7

GLOSSARY OF TRAFFIC CONTROL TERMS

A

ACCESS ROAD - Public roads, existing or proposed, needed to provide essential access to military installation and facilities, or to industrial installations and facilities in the activities of which there is specific defense interest. Roads within the boundaries of military reservation are excluded from this definition unless such roads have been dedicated to public use and are not subject to closure.

ACCIDENT SPOT MAP - An area or installation map showing the location of vehicle accidents by means of symbols. Symbols may represent accidents classified as to daylight hours, night hours, injury or death.

ANGLE PARKING - Parking where the longitudinal axes of vehicles form an angle with the alignment of the roadway.

C

CENTER LINE - A line marking the center of a roadway between traffic moving in opposite direction.

COLLISION DIAGRAM - A plan of an intersection or section of roadway on which reported accidents are diagramed by means of arrows showing manner of collision.

COMBINED CONDITION AND COLLISION DIAGRAM - A condition diagram upon which the reported accidents are diagramed by means of arrows showing manner of collision.

CONDITION DIAGRAM - A plan of an intersection or section of roadway showing all objects and physical conditions having a bearing on traffic movement and safety at that location. Usually these are scaled drawings.

CORDON COUNTS - A count of all vehicles and persons entering and leaving a district (cordon area) during a designated period of time.

CORDON AREA - The district bounded by the cordon line and included in a cordon count.

CROSSWALK - Any portion of a roadway at an intersection or elsewhere distinctly indicated for pedestrian crossing by lines or other markings on the surface. Also, that part of a roadway at an intersection included within the connections of the lateral lines of the sidewalks on opposite sides of the traffic way measured from the curbs, or in the absence of curbs, from the edges of the traversable roadway.

D

DELAY - The time consumed while traffic or a specified component of traffic is impeded in its movement by some element over which it has no control usually expressed in seconds per vehicle.

DESIRE LINE - A straight line between the point of origin and point of destination of a trip without regard to routes of travel (used in connection with an origin-destination study).

DIVIDED STREET - A two-way road on which traffic in one direction of travel is separated from that in the opposite direction by a directional separator. Such a road has two or more roadways.

E

85 PERCENTILE SPEED - That speed below which 85 percent of the traffic unit's travel, and above which 15 percent travel.

F

FIXED-TIME CONTROLLER - An automatic controller for supervising the operation of traffic control signals in accordance with a predetermined fixed time cycle and divisions thereof.

FIXED-TIME TRAFFIC SIGNAL - A traffic signal operated by a fixed-time controller.

FLASHING BEACON - A section of a standard traffic signal head, or a similar type device, having a yellow or red lens in each face, which is illuminated by rapid intermittent flashes.

FLASHING TRAFFIC SIGNAL - A traffic control signal used as a flashing beacon.

FLOATING CAR - An automobile driven in the traffic flow at the average speed of the surrounding vehicles.

FLOW DIAGRAM - The graphical representation of the traffic volumes on a road or street network or section thereof, showing by means of bands the relative volumes using each section of roadway during a given period of time, usually 1 hour.

H

HIGH FREQUENCY ACCIDENT LOCATION - A specific location where a large number of traffic accidents have occurred.

I

INTERSECTION APPROACH - That portion of an intersection leg which is used by traffic approaching the intersection.

L

LATERAL CLEARANCE - The distance between the edge of pavement and any lateral obstruction.

LATERAL OBSTRUCTION - Any fixed object located adjacent to the traveled way which reduces the transverse dimensions of the roadway.

LEFT TURN LANE - A lane within the normal surfaced width reserved for left turning vehicles.

M

MANUAL TRAFFIC CONTROL - The use of-hand signals or manually operated devices by traffic control personnel to control traffic.

MANUAL COUNTER - A tallying device which is operated by hand.

MASS TRANSPORTATION - Movement of large groups of persons.

MULTIAXLE TRUCK - A truck which has more than two axles.

O

OCCUPANCY RATIO -The average number-of occupants per vehicle (including the driver).

ODOMETER -A device on a vehicle for measuring the distance traveled, usually as a cumulative total, but sometimes also for individual trips, with an indicator on the instrument panel where it is usually combined with a speedometer indicator, or in the hub of a wheel in some trucks.

OFF-PEAK PERIOD - That portion of the day in which traffic volumes are relatively light.

OFFSET LANES - Additional lanes used for traffic which is heavier in one direction. Also known as unbalanced lanes.

OFF-STREET PARKING - Lots and garages intended for parking entirely off streets and alleys. street and alleys (may be angle or parallel parking) for parking of vehicles.

ORIGIN DESTINATION STUDIES - A study of the origins and destinations of trips of vehicles and passengers. Usually included in the study are all trips within, or passing through, into or out of a selected area.

OVERALL SPEED - The total distance traversed divided by the travel time. Usually expressed in miles per hour and includes all delays.

OVERALL TIME - The time of travel, including stops and delays except those off the traveled way.

P

PARALLEL PARKING - Parking where the longitudinal axis of vehicles are parallel to alignment of the roadway so that the vehicles are facing in the same direction as the movement of adjacent vehicular traffic.

PARKING DURATION - Length of time a vehicle is parked.

PASSENGER VEHICLE - A free-wheeled, self-propelled vehicle designed for the transportation of persons but limited in seating capacity to not more than seven passengers, not including the driver. It includes taxicabs, limousines, and station wagons, but does not include motorcycles. (In capacity studies, also includes light reconnaissance vehicles, and pickup trucks.)

PASSENGER (TRANSIT) VOLUME - The total number of public transit occupants being transported in a period of time.

PEAK PERIOD - That portion of the day in which maximum traffic volumes are experienced.

PEDESTRIAN - Any person afoot. For purpose of accident classification, this will be interpreted to include any person riding in or upon a device moved or designed for movement by human power or the force of gravity, except bicycles, including stilts, skates, skis, sleds, toy wagons, and scooters.

PERCENT OF GRADE - The slope in the longitudinal direction of the pavement expressed in percent which is the number of units of change in elevation per 100 units of horizontal distance.

PERCENT OF GREEN TIME - The percentage of green time allotted to the direction of travel being studies.

PROPERTY DAMAGE - Damage to property as a result of a motor vehicle accident that may be a basis of a claim for compensation. Does not include compensation for loss of life or for personal injuries.

PUBLIC HIGHWAYS- The entire width between property lines, or boundary lines, of every way or place of which any part is open to use of the public for purposes of vehicular traffic as a matter of right or custom.

PUBLIC TRANSIT - The public passenger carryi ng service afforded by vehicles following regular routes and making specified stops.

R

REFLECTORIZE - The application of some material to traffic control devices or hazards which will return to the eyes of the road user some portion of the light from his vehicle headlights, thereby producing a brightness which attracts attention.

REGULATORY DEVICE - A device used to indicate the required method of traffic movement or use of the public traffic way.

REGULATORY SIGN - A sign used to indicate the required method of traffic movement or use of the traffic way.

RIGHT TURN LANE - A lane within the normal surfaced width reserved for right turning vehicles.

ROADWAY - That portion of a traffic way including shoulders, improved, designed, or ordinarily used for vehicle traffic.

S

SEPARATE TURNING LANE - Added traffic lane which is separated from the intersection area by an island or unpaved area. It may be wide enough for one or two line operation

SHOULDER - The portion of the roadway contiguous with the traveled way for accommodation of stopped vehicles, for emergency use, and for lateral support of base and surface courses.

SIGHT DISTANCES - The length of roadway visible to the driver of a passenger vehicle at any given point on the roadway when the view is unobstructed by traffic.

SIGNAL CYCLE - The total time required for one complete sequence of the intervals of a traffic signal.

SIGNAL CONTROLLER - A complete electrical mechanism for controlling the operation of traffic control signals, including the timer and all necessary auxiliary apparatus mounted in a cabinet.

SIGNAL FACE - That part of a signal head provided for controlling traffic from a single direction.

SIGNAL HEAD - An assembly containing one or more signal faces that may be designated accordingly as one-way, two-way, multi-way.

SIGNAL PHASE - A part of the total time cycle allocated to movements receiving the right-of-way or to any combination ments receiving the right-of-way simultaneously during one

SIMPLE INTERSECTION - An intersection of two traffic ways, approaches.

SPEED - The rate of movement of a vehicle, generally expressed in miles per hour.

STOPPING SIGHT DISTANCE – The distance required by a drive of a vehicle, given speed, to bring vehicle to a stop after and object becomes visible.

STREET WIDTH - The width of the paved or traveled portion of the roadway.

T

THROUGH MOVEMENT - (See THROUGH TRAFFIC)

THROUGH STREET - A street on which traffic is given the right-of-way so that vehicles entering or crossing the street must yield the right-of-way.

THROUGH TRAFFIC - Traffic proceeding through a military installation or portion not originating in or destined to that military installation or portion thereof.

TIME CYCLE - (See SIGNAL CYCLE)

TRAFFIC - Pedestrians, ridden or herded animals, vehicles, street cars, and other conveyances, either singly or together, while using any street for purposes of travel.

TRAFFIC ACCIDENT - Any accident involving a motor vehicle in motion that results in death, injury, or property damage.

TRAFFIC ACTUATED CONTROLLER- An automatic controller for supervising the operation of traffic control signals in accordance with the immediate and varying demands of traffic as registered with the-controller by means of detectors.

TRAFFIC CONTROL - All measures except those of a structural kind that serve to control and guide traffic and to promote road safety.

TRAFFIC CONTROL DEVICE - A Traffic control device is any sign, signal, marking, or device placed or erected for the purpose of regulating, warning, or guiding traffic.

TRAFFIC DEMAND - The volume of traffic desiring to use a particular route or facility.

TRAFFIC ENGINEERING - That phase of engineering that deals with the planning and geometric design of streets, highways, and abutting lands, and with traffic operations thereon, as their use is related to the safe, convenient, and economic transportation of persons and goods.

TRAFFIC FLOW - The movement of vehicles on a roadway.

TRAFFIC FLOW PATTERN - The distribution of traffic volumes on a street or highway network~

TRAFFIC GENERATOR - A traffic producing area such as a post exchange, parking lot, or administrative center.

TRAFFIC SIGNAL INTERVAL - Anyone of the several divisions of the total time cycle during which signal indications do not change.

TRAFFICWAY - The entire width between property lines (or other boundary lines) of every way or place of which any part is open to use of public for purposes of vehicular traffic as a matter of right or custom.

TRANSIT VEHICLE - A passenger carrying vehicle, such as a bus or streetcar which follows regular routes and makes specific stops.

TRAVEL TIME- The total elapsed time from the origin to destination of a trip.

TURNING MOVEMENT - The traffic making a designated turn at an intersection.

TWO-WAY STREETS - A street on which traffic may move in opposite directions simultaneously. It may be either divided or undivided.

TYPE OF ACCIDENT - The kind of motor vehicle accident, such as head-on, right-angle, etc.

TYPE OF SURFACE - The class of surface such as concrete, asphalt, gravel, etc.

U

UNINTERRRUPTED FLOW - The flow of-vehicles under ideal conditions resulting in unrestricted movement.

V

VEHICLE - Every device in, upon, or by which any person or property is or may be transported or drawn upon a highway, except those devices moved by human power or used exclusively upon stationary rails or tracks.

VEHICULE OCCUPANCY - The average number of occupants per automobile, including the driver.

VOLUME - The number of vehicles passing a given point during a specified period of time.

W

WARNING SIGN - A sign used to indicate conditions that are actually or potentially hazardous to highway users.

WARRANT - Formally stated conditions that have been accepted as minimum requirements for justifying installation of a traffic control device or regulation.

Z

ZONE (ORIGIN-DESTINATION STUDIES) -- A division of an area established for the purpose of analyzing origin-destination studies. It may be bounded by physical barriers such as rivers and highways, or may be the location of individual work organizations that have duty stations in relatively close proximity.

www.ingramcontent.com/pod-product-compliance
Lightning Source LLC
Chambersburg PA
CBHW082149300426
44117CB00016B/2668